To Sis / Wymon.

You Exude Class. You
Are A Wonderful Example
of A " Woman of God."
Thank You For Your Love
And Friendship. Your
genuiness is Soooo Refreshing.

Love You Much

[signature]

Staring Down the Barrel of My Faith

Staring Down the Barrel of My Faith

by Pastor Jake Gaines Jr.

Editor

Ray Glandon

Senior Publisher

Steven Lawrence Hill Sr.

Awarded Publishing House

ASA Publishing Company

A Publisher Trademark Title page

ASA Publishing Company
Awarded Best Publisher for Quality Books

(Wayne Commerce Park)
38640 Michigan Avenue, Wayne, Michigan 48184
www.asapublishingcompany.com

Copyrights©2010 Pastor Jake Gaines Jr, All Rights Reserved
Book: Staring Down the Barrel of My Faith
Date Published: 02.09.10 /Edition 1 *Trade Paperback*
Book ASAPCID: 2380537
ISBN: 978-0-9826490-0-8
Library of Congress Cataloging-in-Publication Data

This book was published in the United States of America.
State of Michigan

A Publisher Trademark Title page

Table of Contents

Staring Down The Barrel Of My Faith

By Pastor Jake Gaines Jr.

Introduction

I was led by the Holy Spirit to write this book because of a problem that I believe permeates the Kingdom Of God. That problem is, understanding our faith in God. In my experience, I have seen many people try to use their faith (trust) in God as an excuse to relinquish any responsibility for their spiritual growth and everyday living.

Ephesians 2:8-9:

For it is by grace you have been saved through faith—and this not from yourselves, it is the gift of God—not by works so that no one can boast.

It is clear from Paul's writings that a person is not saved by the works of the law (by living the right way or based on an individual's effort). You are saved by God's unmerited favor, which is grace, through our faith (trust) In God. We cannot do enough good to make ourselves worthy of the reconciliation to God that we have received through the blood of Jesus based on His sacrificial death on the cross. Jesus paid the price, in full, to make us right (atonement) with God.

The phenomenon of being saved is a one-time event through our sincere belief and acceptance that Christ did all that was necessary for us to be redeemed from the penalty and the constant dominance of sin. We simply accept Christ as our Lord and Savior, turn away (repent) from our evil ways and live for Christ.

It is this *living out* of our faith in Christ that I want to focus on in this writing. I want to focus on the practical side of our faith so that others are able to see our faith unto salvation, in our everyday walk and determined it to be authentic. So often, we act as if our faith is a private issue that has nothing to do with what others see in us. This viewpoint is a dangerous and selfish approach to the love that God has shown us. If salvation were only about securing our position in heaven, then it would have been quite appropriate if everyone died the instant they were saved.

We are left here to influence others to receive Christ by the way we live. We are not to view our salvation as a **"for me only"** experience. The way we live has an impact and affect on others as to the choices they make to receive Christ as Lord and Savior.

Faith unto salvation is totally up to God. However, faith manifested in our everyday living is, in major part, our responsibility. Even though it's through the power of the Holy Spirit, we must not consistently resist Him. Others around us should be able to see the results of our salvation. You cannot rightfully declare that you are *saved* while you live an immoral and irreligious life, as if you are an unregenerate.

This, in part, is what the writer James is referring to in James 2:17 "In the same way, faith by itself, if it is not accompanied by action, is dead." If there is no manifestation of your change, then your faith simply cannot be considered authentic. Of what value is it if no one can see it or benefit from it? This makes all the sense in the world. *If you are a teacher, then you should be busy teaching. If you are an honest person, then you should illustrate honesty on a consistent basis. If you are a mechanic, there should be every indication that you are astute in the knowledge of repairing cars.*

We all would be better at exemplifying our faith if we recognize that the manifestation of our faith requires us to roll up our own sleeves and work out the ways of the Lord in our lives, as we allow God to work in us and mold us into His image. If we are truly saved, there will be, at the very least, a true inward desire to learn how to live for God, even when we intermittently struggle. We have a responsibility in the progress of our spiritual growth that should coincide with how sincere we are about our relationship with Jesus Christ and His purpose. We play a major part in this portion of our Christian walk. If you are unwilling to participate in the progress of your own spiritual growth, you place the genuineness of your salvation on the witness stand to be questioned and interrogated. *You simply may not be saved at all.*

People actually attempt to use their faith in God to their personal advantage, to barter with God, instead of using their faith as a foundation. Many Christians use their faith as some kind of magic potion to offset any type of foolish behavior. Then, they attempt to hold God hostage, through His love for us, to rescue them in their time of struggle. There **ARE** consequences to having a faith that is wrapped around underhanded motives.

My objective in this writing is to show that the everyday use of our faith requires us to look at ourselves with a critical eye and ask ourselves if we are truly playing our part in living a holy and productive life to the glory of God.

I am writing from the perspective of **MY** personal experience with **MY** faith in God. I pray it will help anyone whose faith is constantly being challenged by the furtive methods of the devil on a daily basis. I know that my faith in God is genuine, yet I find myself adjusting my attitude and actions each time my faith is challenged. I find that genuine faith is always being tested. *I firmly believe that a faith that cannot be tested cannot be trusted.*

It would be highly hypocritical of me to be overly critical of others' struggles with faith issues when I struggle on a daily basis, myself. This has nothing to do with my struggle with sin; we all have that, but rather with the proper response to an unfailing God in our everyday issues of life. Trusting God with all of my heart is connected more to how I respond to Him in dealing with people on a daily basis, and taking advantage of the many opportunities to edify Him in our response to them.

My faith in God is as closely tied to lifting Him up so others can gain confidence in Him, as it is being obedient to Him. These two elements work in tandem. It's impossible to love God and not care about the plight of the people around you.

My faith in God ought to manifest itself by benefiting other people who come in contact with me and being inspired to seek God due to my commitment to Him.

Each test that God desires me to endure places my faith right before me and makes me see it for what it really is and not for what I imagine it to be. It is amazing how many times a person of faith (me) can fail to respond in the proper manner that would be pleasing to God, and yet it does not negate the fact that my faith is real. What it really does, is makes me realize that my faith in God is the only way that I can truly please HIM because my inability to meet His standards are constantly before me.

I pray that God will continue to shower His mercy upon me, to offset the countless times I have failed Him in my Christian walk. I truly have to *stare down the barrel of my faith* and make honest assessments of my futile attempts to live up to His expectations on an everyday basis. Except for the grace of God in my life, I would be a complete failure in the ways of God.

****

I remember this experience as if it happened yesterday instead of 14 years ago. I was returning from Cleveland, Ohio after both having a marvelous Sunday worshipping and praising God. I had traveled the 180 miles from Cleveland without any problem whatsoever.

As I came within several blocks of my home, I decided to stop at my favorite convenient store to purchase some beverages for the kids. It was approximately 11:30 P.M. Pulling into the parking lot, I had an eerie feeling about how deserted it was. Normally it was bustling with activity. People were usually coming and going all the time.

That eerie feeling was a warning from the Holy Spirit, which I ignored, and it almost cost me my life. In spite of this warning, I rationalized that it would be just a momentary pit stop and all would be well once I ran in and out. Just as I got out of the car, two young thugs appeared out of nowhere brandishing weapons, which were a handgun and a double-barreled shotgun. The shotgun was pointed straight at my forehead, approximately two feet away. The mere fact that this thug chose a shotgun as his weapon of choice indicated that he had no intention of wounding his victim, if compelled to use this destructive weapon. It was a life or death situation.

The words of the young man facing me with the shotgun were clear and precise. *"Give me all of your money or I will blow your!#$%&*) head off."* I was not at all ambivalent about his objective. I was scared out of my wits. I felt that at any moment I would die in this parking lot like an animal, right in front of my family. My thoughts were racing at warp speed, and my mind was void of Bible verses.

I thought to myself, that I had to do something to save my life and protect my children. Being indigenous of the streets myself, I attempted to recall all of things that I learned from my street life that would be of great benefit to me at such a crucial time. I concluded, as I pulled my wallet out of my back pocket, that I would grab the barrel of the shotgun and put up a gallant fight to disarm this demon- possessed youth and let whatever happened after that…. happen. It was going to be him or me.

Keep in mind that all of these thoughts were flowing through my mind in a matter of seconds. A decision needed to be made immediately as this young man became increasingly impatient. "Give it up *&%$#@," he shouted, as he refocused my attention on the severity of the moment. "I will blow your *&%$#@ brains out." I will not die like this. I thought to myself, it's on.

As I reached for my wallet, my grand plan already stabilized in my mind, the Holy Spirit spoke to me with very explicit instructions. *"Look this boy right in the eyes and say to him, you don't know me, and I don't know you, so there is no reason to harm me or my family."'* What? I thought to myself. This demon is not going to listen to any words from God. That's not a good plan at all, I thought secretly to myself. I am going to go down fighting like a *real* man,

The Holy Spirit repeated what He said to me earlier. *"Look this boy right in the eyes and say to him, you don't know me and I don't know you, so there is no reason to harm me or my family."'* What seemed to be an eternity could not have been more than 60 seconds of us staring each other down. Though I knew the Holy Spirit could not mislead me, I struggled to believe that everything would work out for the good. I was strapped with fear. In spite of my trepidation, I chose to obey God.   I looked this shotgun-welding demon straight in the face and said, *"You don't know me, and I don't know you, so there is no reason to harm me or my family."*

Finally, after what seemed to be a lifetime, the cold stare of this demonic-filled teenager turn into a snarl and he coldly replied, "You are right &#$%&!" He slowly lowered the shotgun from between my eyes, as if enjoying every second of my nightmare, and turned away into the darkness. As I jumped into the car to get my family as far away from the scene as I could, all I could say was "Thank you God for saving the lives of my family and me. The tears in my eyes, which were simply a mask for the anger I felt in my mind, were quickly overtaken by the joy I felt for such a miraculous deliverance.

As I look back on that nightmarish night, I realize that something phenomenal had occurred. Not only did God grant me grace through His love, but also I grew up as a child of God. I learned that faith, unlike grace, requires something from me that I sometimes do not want to face, and that is, *honesty about my faith.* I found out that night that my faith requires me to look directly at it and see it for what it really is, not for what I perceive it to be.

As much as I disagreed with what the Holy Spirit said to me, I did it, not because I wanted to, but because my faith required me to look it in the face and make a decision. If you believe God, then act on it. It is up to you. A decision had to be made. I was either going to trust God or myself, but a decision *had* to be made, and it had to be made quickly.

Life has its way, and it's time to make you stare your faith right in the face. What I realized about that night changed my life forever. It was not just that shotgun that was staring me in the face. I was forced to stare down the barrel of my own faith and make a decision. Would I trust God or me? Yes, that night, *I stared down the barrel of my faith,* and made the decision to trust God, and it saved my family and me.

I have found out in my lifetime that faith is not something you simply have a feeling about, it is a response to something. True Christian faith is a response to the sovereignty of God, a response to the control that God has over all things. It is trusting God when you neither want to, nor feel like it.

The reward of faith is based on the power and the purpose of God. It is not how you feel about your circumstances or the results. It is about our response to the faith that we profess. Faith is not based on our emotions, rather, an active response to the trust we declare that we have in God. Though we don't always know what the result of our faith will be, we do know that God will work out a purpose that coincides with HIS will.

When we realize that God has all power to do anything He wants and that He always uses it for the long-range good of humanity, then we can have absolute confidence that we are safe. He has both the ability and the stated purpose of working out all things, including our indifference, rebellion, and blatant disobedience. He is completely trustworthy—worthy of our trust.

I wrote this book so that I could share **MY** response to **MY** faith with you. It is about how through a life-threatening situation, my faith was revealed to me at its least common denominator. I was forced to decide if God was worth trusting in spite of the consequences. I learned so much about my faith in God, which required me to respond to Him in a way that did not agree with me. In spite of how I felt, faith responded with its corresponding result... *the inability to fail.*

To My Wife...Leona

God Sent You To Me

God looked at my flaws
And sent you to me
A loving companion
To help me to be

All He requires
To His glory divine
God knows my needs
Through His holy design

Honest and open
You loved me the same
Keeping me rooted
In God's loving plan

You looked past my faults
To see all my needs
When time kindled doubts
You stayed on your knees

Always God first
Was your pledge of allegiance
Ignoring your hurt
Without rhyme or good reason

I thank God for you
Cause I'm able to see
What a special touch....when
God sent you to me.

I Love You......Jake

Foreword

Pastor Charles D. Twymon,
Macedonia Baptist Church
Detroit, Michigan 48223

There have been a great number of books written on the subject of faith. As a pastor of thirty years, I've read many of those books. Of course, the greatest book ever written on faith is the Bible. I believe the overall theme of the Bible is, *"The just shall live by faith."*

Saving faith and faith in a crisis are not exactly the same thing. We must walk by faith when faith in God makes no sense at all. When your faith in God appears to be diametrically opposed to everything your intellect, your senses, and your experiences tell you, and yet you trust Him and respond in obedience, that's the faith in God that produces a quality of spirit that enables you to face danger and/or pain, in spite of human fears. It produces a courage that says. "God is in control, and I must trust Him."

Living by faith is the main thrust of this book. It's not necessarily the saving faith that brought us into the wonderful relationship we have with God through personal belief in His only begotten Son, Jesus Christ, but a daily active faith. Pastor Jake Gaines Jr. takes a unique approach to the components of faith that surface in our everyday lives.

Every Christian needs to know all that personal faith entails. We all need to ask ourselves if it's possible for fear to frustrate our faith. Can trials or temperament terminate our faith? It is the responsibility of all Christians to operate their lives with total trust in God.

Pastor Gaines clearly separates faith in God from our emotions and helps us understand that faith is not what you feel but how you respond to God. He has taken his own personal life experiences along with what he has encountered in his many years of pastoral guidance and ministry to create this book.

The wisdom in which this book is written should cause readers to re-examine familiar passages of scripture and their own individual faith-walk in the Lord.

This book gives great insight to understanding how your faith can triumph in tribulation and be strengthened through life's struggles.

May this book invoke a reality check and cause you to successfully *stare down the barrel of your own faith.*

Words of Encouragement

Pastor Clifford J. Parker
Christ Temple Missionary Baptist Church
401 University Dr.
Pontiac, Michigan 48342

One of the most enriching and amazing experiences to ever encounter is the submitting of one's life to the written word of Jehovah God (John 3:3-21; Proverb 3:5-10; Psalm 107). This is the only way that a person can experience the heights, depths, dimensions, and dynamics of God's amazing grace and tender mercies.

However, this refined life style, Christianity, is impossible to experience without faith (Hebrews 11:6).

I must admit that at first glance, the title of this book caused me great concern. I had a serious problem with such a title dealing with faith in God. Because of this, I called Pastor Gaines one night about 11:30 P.M. and questioned him about his choice of a title.

Pastor Gaines quickly reminded me of his experience in 1996 and how he was forced to stare down the barrel of his faith and be obedient to God, though he did not agree with what God had told him to do. After this explanation, I no longer had a problem with the title. In fact, I understood it even more.

Every Christian, everyday, must come face to face with his or her faith in God. It is in these mirrors of conflicting experiences that accurately reproduces, describes, and conveys who and what we are.

I have known Pastor Gaines for more than twenty years, and I am convinced of his commitment to God's written word and his love for people. I am honored to be asked to render words of encouragement.

Therefore, to a very dear friend, a trusted and noble brother, and a serious, solemn preacher, pastor, and instructor, Pastor Gaines, you are to be encouraged in all things, and to remain steadfast in the written word of God.

You are a true example of letting others see the work of God flow through you to others. I pray that God will continue to bless you and keep you to His glory and honor as you continue to labor for the cause of Christ, according to His written word.

To My Publisher & President
Steven L. Hill Sr.

Steven, you are not only a talented and innovative leader in the publishing industry, but you are masterful at getting the most out of the least amount of resources.

ASA Publishing Co. might not be a large company, but it looms large in quality and production in the publishing world. I want to thank you for believing in me when you published **"God And My Car."**

Not only have you helped me by educating me in this industry, you have continued to encourage me to press on in spite of the obstacles. Keep striving for excellence, and it will not escape you. You are an inspiration to any new writer who has a desire to have their work published. I thank God for the hard work and dedication that you and your wife Melissa have put into my endeavors.

Though there are times I am intimidated by this writing industry, *you are not,* and your willingness to stand out front and take the blows on my behalf is greatly appreciated.

To My Editor
Ray Glandon

I am absolutely amazed at how personal you take someone else's work. You took my garbled thoughts and gave them clarity and depth. For this I am truly grateful.

You poured yourself into this work, just as you did in **"God And My Car."** Your meticulous method of old fashion editing is a tribute to the dedication that you have for your craft.

You are not only an excellent editor, but you sincerely care about my work and ministry, and it reflects in how you labor to make my manuscript make sense.

I thank God for allowing us to meet you and your wife, Helen, and developing such a wonderful relationship that goes beyond paper and pencil.

Thank you for the many suggestions that paid great dividends in finishing this project. You are truly a gifted professional.

Chapter 1

Faith...The Essential Element To Me Being Whole

In faith there is enough light for those who want to believe and enough shadows to blind those who don't.

Blaise Pascal

Faith unto salvation is an event, while living by faith is a process. Faith unto salvation is a free gift from God. There is no special effort required of you, except to receive Christ as your Lord and Savior and to submit your life to Him. The sincerity of this submission will be determined by the change of behavior in your life through the power of the Holy Spirit that now dwells within you. However, living out this faith is an accumulation of decisions we must make based on our trust in God.

There are few absolutes in life that are more accepted by all cultures and open to more social and economic differences while being blind to racial barriers than these three.

Faith
Love
Hope

Faith is what I would like to focus on because I believe it is the one we seem to pay the least attention to and the one most misunderstood. Faith in God is the key element to being whole, to being brought back from the brink of mental terror or physical disability, two experiences that affect the relationship between man and God.

Faith, love and hope are all measurable by degrees. Faith, however, has a unique distinction in that it alone has no motive other than to be an empowering agent to hope and love. No matter how much God loves you, you still have to believe and trust (faith) that He does. Take love for instance. There is a need to have it returned to the one who initiates it, with equal or greater value, so that the initiator feels validated in offering it in the first place.

Love is a building block to any relationship, but it takes a spark of "Hope" from within to establish a belief system, that both parties can be trusted. Faith therefore, is believing in someone or something and then depending on the initiating party of this love, to be genuine in their claim. We can trust in the love of God. He is perfect and cannot deceive us.

We must realize that we are the Achilles Heel in our relationship with God. We are the ones who fail Him, not God failing us. God's faithfulness to us ought to generate confidence in our faith toward Him. Trusting is the linchpin to our relationship with God. If we do not trust Him, we will always underestimate the value of knowing Him. This will circumvent our efforts to having a true intimate relationship with God.

We as human beings inherently trust in something or someone. Even a newborn baby has a built in trust system that has been nurtured by nine months of dependency on someone else. That infant will willingly open his or her mouth to be fed, without any knowledge of what's being fed. The child is born dependent on someone else to sustain him. It's imperative, however, that the dominant party of this relationship is both loving and honest in order for the dependent party to be nourished and looked after in a loving and productive way. Nearly everyone trusts in someone or something to meet his or her general needs.

It is a comforting thought to know that we, as Christians, have someone other than ourselves that we can trust and depend on to look after our needs. While others may call this some kind of force or energy, we know from the Bible that it is an all-powerful God that we have a personal relationship with, who created us and sustains us.

Because we know that God is a perfect God, who is incapable of failing, we grow more comfortable each day in allowing Him to govern our lives in a way that can never be reserved for anyone else. The longer we live, the more we realize how much and how often we have had to depend on the love and faithfulness of someone other than ourselves. Whether we believe in the true and Living God or not, we've had to live with some degree of faith in something or someone.

More often than not, people do not want to appear weak and dependent on anything other than themselves, and they refuse to connect any religious connotation to an act of faith. However, to believe in anything outside of yourself for sustenance is, in and of itself, an act of religiosity; it's just a matter of what you believe in. Those of us who have experienced a personal relationship with God through our Lord and Savior Jesus Christ have identified that outside source as God and recognize that He is the source of all that we are and the sustenance of our being.

It is clear to us that God does not benefit from His relationship with us. God is not enhanced nor influenced in any way by having this personal relationship with us. Because He is sovereign, being in total control of everything, He is the initiator and the sustainer of this relationship, and we are totally dependent upon Him. He is neither made better by His goodness nor worse by His judgments. He is just a perfect God, and we can only know Him by His willingness to reveal Himself to us.

Faith is so essential, that God gives everyone the opportunity to accept and acknowledge Him through it. Faith is the channel through which someone who is invisible to us can become viable for us. Though faith and facts often collide violently, it is faith that turns curiosity into confidence. It is faith that allows God to react to us in a way that cannot be defined as conjecture because it makes the invisible….visible.

Isn't it interesting that people are willing to trust *"chance,"* rather than believe that there is a true and living God that is in total control of everything, who will allow you to have a relationship with Him? It's rather amusing that no matter how many times *"chance"* fails us, and that's about 99.9% of the time, we are still willing to give it another chance. (*I could not resist that pun*)

We inherently need to trust something or someone because it becomes abundantly clear early in our cognitive understanding that there are just too many things that we can't do for ourselves, too many circumstances we simply cannot control. This lack of control leaves us feeling fragmented, frustrated, and alienated so frequently in our lives.

One of the essential elements of feeling whole is that we have someone we can depend on when we are perplexed and uneasy. It's very comforting to know that God, who is able to help us, is also willing to help us. How encouraging is that? Though God will say no sometimes, to our requests because they are not in line with His will it's never because He does not love us. I always tell people that *"I would rather serve a God who can, but might not, than to serve a God who might, but cannot."*

Each experience with God is a building block for our faith to develop. Good or bad, we become more familiar with the methods of God. The more familiar we are with God's methods, the more confidence we have in Him. The more confidence we have, the more we will trust Him. When we put our trust in God, it lessens the chances of us feeling hopeless, even when we are helpless. We can live our lives realizing that no matter when God intervenes, something good and glorious will result from it.

Our wholeness, as people, is often tied to how much control we have over our circumstances. We are often defined by the control we have to create change, and we are looked upon with disdain when we are found to be submissive. It's as if we must at all times be in total control to validate our existence.

The fact is, there are so many things that we have absolutely no control over, we often lose our zest for life. I don't mean we become uselessly depressed or anything of that nature, but we have a tendency to give less than our best to God because we don't believe that the end result can really make a profound difference. We define God based upon what is going on in our lives instead of redefining our circumstances by our relationship with God, who is in complete control. We have a tendency to blame God for our messes. We feel that God ought to be compassionate enough to simply fix things, in spite of our indifference toward Him.

So much of our fragmentation comes from having so much faith in people. This is a direct result of not having enough faith in God. If we trusted God more than we trusted people, people would not become the line of demarcation that defines who we are. Our euphoria would not be as great when people approve, and our disappointments would not be as debilitating when they don't.

So much of the disenchantment among people of God is related to the unwillingness to accept how different we may be in spite of our love for God. We need to understand that our commonality is in Christ, not necessarily in the way we do or see things. Everyone might not like you or agree with you, but it does not define who you are. You may not be looked upon with the highest regard, or understood, or loved by the masses. This, however, does not correctly define God's love and purpose for you. In the 23rd Psalm David said, "He prepares a table for me in the presence of my enemies." God can, and will bless you in spite of your critics and in spite of the odds.

What God has for you, no one can stop. I often ask my congregation why would you hold a grudge against your enemy when God has allowed you to rise above them. If God has allowed you to rise above the taunts of your enemy, then let the grudge go. People do not have to love you for you to love them in return, through the power of the Holy Spirit. Vengeance is God's and not ours. Not only is it ungodly, it's unproductive.

If this were the case, then your love for them is predicated upon what they can do for you and not based on what God is doing through you. This line of thinking tends to take away from your wholeness as a person because you are constantly trying to determine what is wrong with you. This will keep you from recognizing that God can and will do a great work in you if you focus on Him. We spend too much of our lives as Christians vying for other people's validation and ignoring God. This will always keep you from recognizing what God is doing in you. You will always feel incomplete and fragmented, relegated to hiding behind shallow "amen's" and conjured up "halleluiahs" in the church sanctuary.

We are simply too enamored with acceptance from other people. We are more willing to take on someone else's opinion of us than our own, not to mention what God thinks of us. Isn't that a frightening thought? We actually put more validity in what another person thinks than what God says. The irony is that the very acceptance that we desire from others is actually coming from people with their own set of defects. It actually boils down to the flawed evaluating the flawed.

Our wholeness can only be found in the bosom of God. It is His truth that makes us free (John 8:31). This is due to the fact that it is an absolute truth that is not tainted by the whims of others with ulterior motives. God does not profit from us, and what He says is never motivated by what He can get out of it. It's for our benefit alone. We can depend on it. We can trust it. We can rely on its purity.

Faith in God is that entity in our life that allows us to rest in the bosom of someone that has the ability to see what we cannot. Therefore, we do not have to take our mistakes as the bottom line factor that determines who we are. God has defined His people. He has declared that we belong to Him through the blood of Jesus Christ, so when we sin against God we certainly should be grieved by our mistakes, but not destroyed by them. Our faith in what Jesus did for us on the cross should instill a renewed fervor in us to bounce back and prove the indwelling of the Holy Spirit by the change in our lives. Our ability to be boldly resilient should be a visible characteristic.

It is this constant awareness that improvement is always just around the corner if we trust what God is doing in us. If we are sincere in our efforts to please God, then we are never faced with more than a *crossroads* in our lives, never a *dead end.* God has the answer. The question is, will we take the time to hear Him?

Faith is a very simple concept; **Trust God.** Imagine how much time we spend trying to figure God out. Why this, God? Why that, God? What's really funny is that we wind up not figuring Him out anyway, so why not start just trusting Him? Haven't you put enough trust in yourself? While faith is simple, people are complex. So much of who and what we are cannot readily be seen until it becomes an action that must now be processed and evaluated; therefore, we are constantly walking on egg shells wondering what we will have to deal with next.

Faith in God reminds us that we are prepared for the hand that life might deal us, though we may not like it. In Jesus we have defeated Satan's greatest weapon, which is death. If we can overcome the grave, we can overcome anything. Though we all fear tragedies in our lives, isn't it a wonderful thing to know that whatever might come our way, God will not forsake us or evaluate us based on those circumstances? Our wholeness is still in His hands regardless of how helpless we may be. What a comforting thought, don't you think?

1st Corinthians. 15:54-58 (NIV)

^{54}When the perishable has been clothed with the imperishable, and the mortal with immortality, then the saying that is written will come true: "Death has been swallowed up in victory." ^{55}"Where, O death, is your victory?

Where, O death, is your sting?" ^{56}The sting of death is sin, and the power of sin is the law. ^{57}But thanks be to God! He gives us the victory through our Lord Jesus Christ. ^{58}Therefore, my dear brothers, stand firm. Let nothing move you. Always give yourselves fully to the work of the Lord, because you know that your labor in the Lord is not in vain.

When we clearly internalize the fact that we no longer have to fear life's nuclear bomb (death), then life itself becomes less stressful. Jesus has defeated death, yet we die spiritually of broken hearts over things that will not matter for any significant amount of time.

So many broken people are those who profess to be saved and sanctified for the use of Christ. Their Christianity is like the lid on a pot that hides the smell of spoiled food. They are still controlled by debilitating thoughts. They are still encased in the same attitudes. They still see life through the eyes of a prisoner. These people just cannot grasp the freedom that they now have through the blood of Jesus to cast off the fears and apprehensions of being who others think they should be. We are freed from the encasement of other people's opinions and philosophy. We are purposed by the will of God and not the folly of men. It does not matter if we are ever famous, or rich, or accepted by the ways of a carnal people.

Our faith in God must assure us that we are on the right track because we are doing it God's way, and that can only bring the results God wants. We are too preoccupied with letting our circumstances define how we are doing. Our circumstances merely measure how life is dealing with us, not God. Even in the worst of circumstances God will declare that we are victors when our circumstances scream out failure. We are victors because we are in the will of God. This means we are safe. We are victors because we have a true relationship with the Almighty God. We are victors because we have overcome the devil through the Word of God.

So much of the emptiness and fragmentation that we feel is a result of trying to love God one way and love people another. We must genuinely love people because God tells us to and not because of how they treat us. Our love for people is the visible manifestation of God's love toward us. It simply flows through us to others. It amazes me how people actually believe that they are in the will of God but do not care how they influence other human beings. We cannot feel one way about God and another way about the people we impact.

Think about this for a minute. Why do we look for wholeness in things that are actually fragmented themselves? If something does not last forever, then it too, is not actually whole (complete), whether it is a person, a thing, or a situation. What ultimately occurs is that we are constantly re-evaluating who we are every time we have to start all over again in any of life's situations.

A major part of your wholeness is determined by how you affect other people. Do you at least make them curious about the love of God based on your faithfulness in God and your love for them? Instead, are you the kind of person who repels them from God because of what they see in you? Your faith in God is never disassociated from your relationship with people because it is your faith (trust) in the ways of God that will get you beyond the disappointment that people will often bring into your life.

It is your faith in God that will not allow you to quit on people who are not where you are spiritually. So many of the people that we shy away from, because they have habits that we don't approve of, often have less malice in their hearts than we do. It is our faith that will help develop the wholeness that we seek in this life. It is our faith, because that is our trust in God, not in people's responses. We cannot find wholeness in this life if it does not include the tandem of God first and then people.

Doesn't it make more sense to seek your wholeness from the source that will last forever? If anyone knows and understands what wholeness is, it would be God, The Alpha and the Omega, the beginning and end of all things. It would seem to make a lot of sense to put your trust in God and let Him define who you are and direct your ways of life.

By the way ..... How well have you done with your life? Personally, mine was a mess, fronting and pretending that everything was just great, when the truth of the matter was I was consumed by trying to be what I was not, that is, until I began to truly trust God. God **IS** the answer to you understanding who you are. Seek your wholeness in Him and Him alone. Everything else is temporary anyway.

My Faith Has Made Me Whole

All around me I see fragments
Of my growth scattered about
Decisions that I regret
Shortcomings stand and shout

They remind me of my futility
To do life on my own
As I fight the demons deep within
As I struggle toward the throne

Of God that calls me to holiness
A life that ought to reflect
The grace that I've received from Him
Swallows my neglect

I fail, and I fail again
I pray from knees well bent
As I struggle hard to fight the sin
That Satan so well sent

I realize that in all I do
I have no right to claim
That I am something by myself
For that is not my aim

It is my trust in God
That leads me to my peace
Because I lay in His embrace
It sets my mind at ease

I am all that I am in God
I truly can't bestow
Any credit upon myself
It's my faith that makes me whole.

By Jake Gaines Jr.

Chapter 2

Building My Faith One Experience At A Time

"Faith exists when absolute confidence in that which we cannot see combines with action that is in absolute conformity to the will of our Heavenly Father. Without all three--first, absolute confidence; second, action; and third, absolute conformity— without these three all we have is a counterfeit, a weak and watered-down faith."
                              --Joseph B. Wirthlin

I clearly recall a winter when we had an unusual amount of snowfall. It seemed that every other day it was snowing. One day in particular we received approximately ten inches of snow overnight, so you can imagine the havoc we experienced that next morning.

Cars were stuck in snow all over the complex. I thought to myself, who would have thought this much snow could accumulate from those little tiny snowflakes. It was mind boggling how this mass of snow could be produced, one snowflake at a time.

As I thought back on the night before, I clearly remembered how all of this started. I recalled watching as one snowflake fell after another. Some flakes were larger than others, each with its unique shape and personality. Some fell gently to the ground while others plummeted to earth with as much velocity as a snowflake could possibly muster. They all fell differently, yet they found their destination.

Some snowflakes fell without much hindrance while others were wind blown up against cars and buildings. Some landed on people as they walked in the snowstorm. Some flakes were stepped upon and obliterated. Some fell alone to the ground while others latched onto other falling snowflakes and reached the ground connected to one another as if the strong were assisting the weak.

By morning, approximately 10 inches of snow had fallen. The accumulation of all those snowflakes had brought our community to a screeching halt. There were snowdrifts five feet tall, and it was a monumental task just to get to your car, not to mention trying to drive it. It was simply astonishing how so many tiny and seemingly insignificant snowflakes could become such a major force when brought together over a period of time.

As I sat watching the events unfold, it occurred to me that this is the same way God builds your belief and trust (faith) in Him on an everyday basis. The cognitive part of our faith is a decision we determine to make. The practical side of our faith is a process reflected over a period of time. By this, I mean that you can decide to start believing God in an instant. You can make a cognitive choice to let God lead your life by allowing Him to come into your life as your Lord and Savior and guide your life according to His will and His way.

This you can do at any time and place in your life. *Hopefully, it will be today.* You then need to find a Bible teaching and preaching church to attend regularly so that you can be trained and nurtured in your Christian journey. God will then begin to live inside of you through the Holy

Spirit and guide and empower you to overcome the sins that have had dominion over you up until this time. He will forgive you for all of your evil and make you a new creature, and you can start your life all over again as a child of God, forgiven and redeemed. You now have a relationship with God that is secured by the blood that Jesus shed on the cross for the sins of mankind. All of this is procured in an instant, when you receive Christ as your Savior.

The flip side of this coin is building your faith in a practical way. Your faith unto salvation is an event, but, the process of you trusting God in your everyday life is an accumulation of experiences with God that prove to you that He is who He says He is. This takes time and patience.

The Bible says; *"Taste and see that the LORD is good; blessed is the man who takes refuge in him."* (Psalm 34:8) It is an invitation to experience God one on one. You need to draw your own conclusions about God through personal experiences over a sustained period of time.

Many people try God to get what they want out of the experience. This is a grave error because you only see God through the outcome of the circumstances that may have driven you to Him. If these circumstances do not change quickly enough for you, or in your perception, work out in your favor, you will judge God based on the outcome of the circumstances, and that judgment will usually turn out to be wrong.

Just as the snowflakes fell gently overnight to accumulate the morning mass of snow, each and every one of your experiences with God ought to ultimately build an avalanche of faith. You will not trust God on an everyday basis unless you experience Him continuously. Your faith will become more prevalent over an extended period of time.

Each experience with God is a building block of practical faith. Each time God responds to you in your life, it ought to build a greater trust in Him that causes you to continue to have confidence in Him. If God is unfamiliar to you, you will not trust Him as much as you would if you had a previous track record with Him. *To know God is to trust God. To trust God is to know God.* The more you know about the way He works, the more you have confidence that He will respond as only the true and living God can. This does not mean He responds as you want, rather, He will respond as the sovereign (in total control) God that He is.

You must be willing to go through the process of experiences that are required for YOU to lean and depend on God. Like the snowflakes, each experience has its own purpose. Each experience has its own personality. These experiences are designed for you to see God in various aspects so that you are able to experience the magnificence of God in your life. All of your experiences may not be mine, and all of my experiences may not be yours. You can't judge your experiences with God based on how He responds to someone else. You have to trust Him for yourself. It is up to God to decide what each of us needs to be and what He wants us to be as it relates to His design and purpose.

Most people will not endure the experiences with God that are necessary to fully trust Him with unalterable confidence. They see God as this instantaneous panacea to their problems. They want God to fix the problems in their life but are not truly concerned with a relationship with Him. People spend years living without a relationship with

God while their lives develop into a ball of confusion and chaos and then we demand that God fix it overnight if He wants us to be faithful in this relationship. Well, guess what? It simply does not work that way. It is not God who needs a relationship with us, but instead, *WE* need a relationship with God. We are in no position to barter with God. We have nothing to offer in trade.

To properly barter, each party must offer the other something of value that is needed or wanted. What do you have to offer God that He needs or wants? Why should God trade off anything with you? What can you give Him that will make Him better? I can answer that for you.......*NOTHING!!!* God simply loves us enough to want a personal relationship with us. We should be so appreciative that God wants to commune with us, that nothing else should even matter. Just imagine, God wants a relationship with me, with all of my faults and shortcomings.

Abram was divinely selected as the forefather of the nation of Israel and had established a remarkable relationship with God through a myriad of experiences along the journey of life. It is not clear how old Abram was at the time God initially established this relationship with him. At the start of this relationship, Abram was living with his wife, Sarai, in the Mesopotamian city of Ur. Abraham was instructed to leave his country and his people and to go to a place that was totally unfamiliar to him.

Genesis 12:1-3

> *"Go forth from your country, and from your relatives and from your father's house, to the land which I will show you; and I will make you a great nation, and I will bless you, and make your name*

great; and so you shall be a blessing; and I will bless those who bless you, and the one who curses you I will curse. And in you all the families of the earth shall be blessed"

Armed with that potent promise, Abram pulled up stakes, and with his father Terah, his nephew Lot, and his wife Sarai, he began the long trek northward around the fertile crescent to the city of Haran. They tarried in Haran until Terah, Abram's father, died. Once again God tells Abram to leave and head toward the country that God chose for him to possess. Isn't it amazing what God will ask of us in spite of our unfamiliarity with Him? God does not have to explain why He wants us to respond to Him as God. God has a greater plan for us than we can understand. God will arbitrarily decide when to test the faith that we have.

God has the prerogative to challenge our faith as He sees fit, and this is exactly what He does with Abram. God required Abram to trust Him when He stated that Abram would have a promised son, even though he was already seventy five years old at the time the promise was given. What an amazing task to ask of this man, and yet this trust would increase, in time, in spite of Abram's faults and disobedience. God presented himself to Abram in a way that Abram was comfortable in trusting Him, and he endured the hardships of uprooting. Though Abram's trust was not perfect, whose is? He followed God.

Let's look at portions of this process that caused Abram's confidence in God to increase, in spite of the fact that his own faith was not perfect.

✝ Abram (before his named was changed to Abraham) resides in Haran with his father until God speaks to him and tells him to leave his familiar surroundings.

✝ God tells Abram to go into Canaan, but he continues into Egypt, gets into trouble, and has to lie about Sarai being his wife so that his life would not be in jeopardy. God delivers him in spite of this disobedience.

✝ There was strife between Abram and his nephew Lot once they got into the land of Canaan. For the sake of peace, Abram, though entitled, took the least fertile land that was available, and God blessed him.

✝ Abram had to rescue his nephew Lot, who was taken into captivity by Mesopotamian kings.

✝ God makes a covenant with Abram regarding having a child of his own loins, (Abram was seventy-five and Sarai was sixty-five, and Abram believed Him, and it was counted as righteousness.

✝ Abram had major strife in his house between his wife and his maid servant, Hagar, who had bore him a child. Sarah, taking matters into her own hands, had grown impatient and gave her maid-servant to Abram to bear a child for him on her behalf. Abram went along with it. (Abram was then 86 years old.)

✝ At 99 years of age God appears to Abram again and promises that he will have a great progeny that could not be counted, and He changes his name to **Abraham**, and Sarai's name to **Sarah.**

✝ God kept His covenant. The Promised Son (Isaac) was born when Abraham was 100 and Sarah was 90 years old. This occurred some twenty five years after the promise was initially made. You talk about having faith in God…..Wow!

It is clear that our faith in God is affected by the personal experiences we have with Him. Abraham's faith (trust) in God grew in direct proportion to his everyday experiences with God. It's interesting how some people literally expect their faith in God to grow without knowing Him personally and interacting with Him (through prayer and the Word of God) on a regular basis. Many people really believe that their faith can grow instinctively without cognitive thought and work. It's as if somehow faith grows out of nothingness without a source or a purpose.

Let's also explore the continuing struggles of faith. Faith grows best the more it has to be experienced. The more your faith is challenged, the greater the quality of your faith will become. The person who prays for God to remove all of the obstacles and challenges in their life is also asking for a sickly spiritual life. Sometimes our faith falters under stress, but if we admit the failure and accept God's forgiveness, even those failures can contribute to our spiritual growth. Abraham and Sarah are both commended for their great faith in Scripture, but their failures are recorded for our instruction and encouragement.

Believe it or not, for the Christian, *faith and failings* often travel in pairs. It is our failings that constantly remind us that we need our faith in God expressed in our lives daily. *People of great faith, in the Bible, often faiedl copiously.* It is through our human failures that our faith is often fortified and through our faith that our failures become vivid to us. By this, I mean that our human failures often put us into positions that cause us a lot of stress and grief. Our faith in the forgiveness of God, for mistakes we make, is paramount to our recovery. We must truly trust that if we are sincere in our repentance, that God will forgive us and allow us to start all over again, living our lives for Him. In spite of how grievous the circumstances are, or what the ultimate consequences may be, God's love for us is the catalyst to our new beginning. Our human failures ought to show us that faith in ourselves only... is futile and we need to lean and depend on Jesus Christ to sustain us.

Proverbs 3:5-8 informs us of the blessing in trusting God.

> *5 Trust in the LORD with all your heart and lean not on your own understanding; 6 in all your ways acknowledge him, and he will make your paths straight. 7 Do not be wise in your own eyes; fear the LORD and shun evil. 8 This will bring health to your body and nourishment to your bones. (NIV)*

Each experience we have with God should add to our foundation of faith just as each snowflake accumulated became a huge snow bank. This happens over a period of time. Each experience shows us God from a different perspective. It is ludicrous to believe that a handful of life's experiences could possibly paint a clear picture of the vastness of God. To know everything that has ever been written about God, is still to know very little about Him. That's just how awesome He is.

Remember, our practical everyday faith in God is an accumulation of our experiences with God. It does not happen overnight. Therefore, stay encouraged even when you struggle with your faith. It does not necessarily mean that you are disconnected, but rather, it is an indication that God may be too far out of your view based on your lack of experiences with Him in an intimate and continuous setting.

It is imperative that we allow God to work in our lives within His time frame and not ours. Remember, you cannot barter with God. Neither you nor I have anything of value to *cut a deal* with God. You have to decide at some time or another that *you are going to be totally committed to God.*

We must realize that it's not about us, but about what God wants for us. We must ask God to help us to trust Him and allow the experiences in our lives to strengthen our relationship with Him as we watch Him work in and through our daily encounters while He fulfills His purpose in our lives.

Each new experience with God teaches us more about His character and His essence. It lets us know who we are dealing with and how He relates to us as His creation.

Remember, don't judge God by the severity of your circumstances, but instead, judge your circumstances by the veracity of God. It's important to allow your experiences with God to accumulate over a sustained period of time and you determine that He is all that the Word of God says He is.

Experience

Where did you come from
With such authority
To manifest when you desire
Oft overwhelming me?

Why must you be my teacher?
Why can't I just be told?
Why can't I live my life my way
And let it just unfold?

Who gave you permission
To seek me out to see
If I have learned anything
From my adversity?

"I am who I am,"
Experience declared.
"I do this by design
Not to be compared

To anything you've ever seen
Or ever felt before.
I'm Experience, and you must glean
The knowledge I have stored."

So, I've learned that Experience
Is wisdom in disguise
It's my conclusion ever since
Experience made me wise

For I am truly fallible
There's so much more to see
Experience is valuable
It brings out the best in me.

By Jake Gaines Jr.

Chapter 3

When My Faith And My Anxiety Must Co-Exist

A little faith will bring your soul to heaven; a great faith will bring heaven to your soul. " -- Charles Spurgeon

We often speak of having faith in something or someone; however, too often there is no active response that coincides with our declaration. It is the response to your faith which actually determines the depth of your faith. Faith is actually a belief that is intertwined with an action.

Christian faith is defined as:

A belief in or a confident attitude toward God, involving commitment to His will for one's life.

How often we claim to have faith while we sit passively and live below our godly potential. We are so often governed and evaluated by the circumstances that surround us. We are seldom aroused by the sovereignty of God. We seem to forget that He is in constant and complete control of this universe, which includes our lives. No matter what malady we may be experiencing, God has a divine purpose to be fulfilled. This is where many Christians fall by the wayside. Somewhere between our faith and our experiences, our zeal for God gets swallowed up, like the Bluewater Guppy being devoured by the great Baleen Whale in one gulp. When the negative elements of life find comfort on our doorsteps, we often compare our immediate circumstances to our perceived faith and find them to be incompatible.

I cannot count the times when I felt that the hardships I had to endure were not fair, based on my love for God, and my faithfulness to His service. *What a grand view I had of myself!* Like anyone else, I found myself asking, why me? Instead of, what is God's purpose? What we actually mean is, Lord I don't deserve this, therefore, put it on someone else. I began to interrogate God regarding His choices of experiences to use to help me grow. We tend to like what our faith in God will do *for* us, but we quiver at the thought of what our faith in God must do *to* us. For God to use us at our maximum efficiency, we must allow Him to change our character so that it is more like His. This requires us to *"look down the barrel of our faith"* and determine just how genuine our faith in God really is. I have found mine to be so inadequate at times, in spite of my love for Him.

The very definition of faith is also the requirement of faith. That requirement is to trust God no matter what happens. We don't have to like God's methods of operation or agree with it, but we do have to trust God in spite of how we feel.

Keep in mind, faith is not agreeing with God, but trusting Him. Sometimes bad things do happen to good people. There are times when personal circumstances appear to be unfair and unjust from a moral standpoint, but from God's perspective, it is often necessary, through trying times, to remind man of the horrible decision Adam made to disobey God and usher sin, death, disease, and immorality, etc. into our lives. It is a constant reminder that we need God to be active in our lives, just to make this existence worthwhile and understandable.

We may find ourselves at odds with God emotionally since He accomplishes His purposes by using methods that we just cannot comprehend. We must trust God even when we do not feel that we have been treated fairly by Him, when defined by the circumstances that surround us. *God's decisions do not have to include an explanation.*

You might ask yourself how you can feel like your faith is real when you are really mad at God, or at the very least you find yourself perplexed by Him. You might think, how can my faith and my anxiety co-exist? Isn't that being a hypocrite? If I have faith in God, shouldn't I always be pleased with His decisions? If I have faith in God, shouldn't I always be confident and unafraid? The answer is… not necessarily. It is not your pleasure with God or your individual bravery that determines your faith in God, it is your continued commitment to His will and His way. Faith is not always proceeding without fear; it is however, trusting God in spite of your fear.

Many of the most faithful men of God were often at odds with Him regarding His methods and decisions. Many of these great men simply had to overcome their differences with God, or at the very least, rise above their fears and press on. Moses made no bones about disagreeing with God in terms of facing the Pharaoh of Egypt and telling him to let God's people go. In spite of what he thought was a valid excuse not to do God's will, which was his speech impediment, Moses still obeyed God, but it was with much trepidation, yet he ultimately led the nation of Israel to freedom. Gideon showed great fear and concern pertaining to God's command to fight the great Medianite army, despite being the least in his father's tribe. In spite of his fear, he obeyed God and conquered them. David fled in fear of the maniacal pursuit of Saul, who intended to kill him. The profit Elijah hid from King Ahab's henchmen because the King's wife, Jezebel, had ordered Elijah to be assassinated. He feared for his life but Elijah obeyed God's instructions, as puzzling as they may have been.

I have come to acknowledge that anxiety and faith often have to co-exist because we have so many flaws and both fear and faith have their own distinctive purpose. Our anxieties should be constant reminders to us that we do not have control over the things that are often so important to us. How appropriate it is that God is love and the creator of life, our two most important elements. Why then, do we consider consulting everyone else before we talk to God regarding these two subjects? Nobody can give us the insight that God can, so why waste valuable time?

Our anxieties, are often the residue of a lack of control. If we could control the circumstances that cause us discomfort, we would not have the discomfort in the first place. Let us make sure we do not confuse intermittent anxiety with constant worry. When we speak of anxiety we are referring to a temporary emotional state of uneasiness, waiting on the deliverance of God, based on our faith in Him, as opposed to an attitude of worry because of our inability to have control of our circumstances.

In 2 Corinthians 12:7-10 Paul tells us of the torment he had with his thorn in the flesh. Even though scholars differ on what that thorn was, the point from God is not lost. Paul was tormented by this physical malady, which certainly caused this man of faith to have great anxieties because of it, yet he did not quit trusting God in spite of his circumstances, which had to co-exist with his faith. Faith makes you do, even if it's just the *waiting* that you are doing.

It is in our weaknesses, our inability to change things we do not like, that God's power stands out because we know that we could not have gotten through the ordeal without God sustaining us. Therefore there is no need for us to boast about anything.

When I am anxious about something, it truly makes me focus on the power of God and directs me, willing or not, to the faith I have declared to possess. It is not that I desire to be anxious; just that I know some experiences in life will bring about this negative emotion because of my inability to be sovereign, as only God is.

Sometimes we are forced to turn to our faith simply because there is nothing within our power that can help us. When we turn to our faith, we simultaneously turn our attention toward God. *It is God we must trust, not our faith itself....* Wow! This blows my mind. Unbelievably, some people simply have faith in their faith as opposed to having faith in God. When your faith is in your faith, you have serious doubts about the ultimate outcome when that faith wavers, but when you have your faith directed toward God, you know He will not fail you no matter how much you disagree with his method.

It is crucial that we do not let our fears change the object (focal point) of our faith. We must keep our faith focused on the power of God and not our own capabilities to perform.

When anxiety does overtake you on occasion, you must take away its strength by recognizing that you are required to fight in the strength of the Lord. Remember again what God ultimately told Paul in a time of anxiousness after he prayed three times for the thorn in his flesh to be removed.

2 Corinthians 12:7-10

> *[7]To keep me from becoming conceited because of these surpassingly great revelations, there was given me a thorn in my flesh, a messenger of Satan, to torment me. [8]Three times I pleaded with the Lord to take it away from me. [9]But he said to me, "My grace is sufficient for you, for my power is made perfect in weakness." Therefore I will boast all the more gladly about my weaknesses, so that Christ's power may rest on me. [10]That is why, for Christ's sake, I delight in weaknesses, in insults, in hardships, in persecutions, in difficulties. For when I am weak, then I am strong.*

Even though it is not by God's design that we worry, we do suffer from occasional and sometimes perpetual anxieties because we are creatures of habit, and sudden changes in our lives often leave us unprepared and vulnerable. This is when our faith must co-exist with our anxieties because many times they exist simultaneously whether we want to admit it or not. We then must fight in the strength of the Lord as we recognize our inability to immediately change our situation. We can actually take what looks to be a liability and turn it into an asset. In spite of our anxiousness, our faith can still be quite effective because its effectiveness is not based on our emotions but rather on our commitment to exercise it. If you must always wait to overcome your fears to believe that your faith is genuine, how then, do you revert to your faith in time of crisis, when fear is all around you?

Many times Christians, in a feeble effort to glorify God or simply to be impressive to others, will boast about their faith and base the boasting on the fact that they do not fear anything because they trust God. Not only is this unnecessary to illustrate faith in God, I just do not believe it. All of us, who love the Lord, still fear some things in this life. Whatever it is for you, may not apply to me. However, make no mistake about it, there are some situations in my life as a Pastor which have rendered me speechless because of my fear, and this may not apply to you. In spite of my anxieties, I realized that my faith in God could and would sustain me, notwithstanding my trepidation. I sincerely believe we mislead people by having them believe that we exist without any fear at all. We place ourselves on an ecclesiastical pedestal that's beyond the reach of others. We leave them feeling as if they are beyond help. We must be careful to let people know that, in spite of being people of God, with a divine purpose ordained for our lives, we still find ourselves digging our way out of the abyss of fear from time to time.

Remember, we are not rewarded based on how we feel about our faith, but instead on how we respond to it. We are still obligated through our faith to let God finish the work that He has started in us. We must never give up, regardless of how many times we desire to do so. We must let our faith be the driving force toward the presence of God and fight through our anxieties until we see our faith fulfilled in the will of God.

I was talking on the telephone with my friend and colleague, Pastor Charles Twymon__ *that's right, he is the one who wrote the foreword.* This profound man of God has been an absolute blessing to me in my ministry, for the last twenty years. Well, while Pastor Twymon was talking to me, he brought out an interesting point that I want to share with you. Man! I wish I was this smart. In the Gospel of Luke 5:1-7 (KJV) you will find these words.

Luke 5:1-7

> *1 And it came to pass, that, as the people pressed upon him to hear the word of God, he stood by the lake of Gennesaret,*
> *2 And saw two ships standing by the lake: but the fishermen were gone out of them, and were washing their nets.*
> *3 And he entered into one of the ships, which was Simon's, and prayed him that he would thrust out a little from the land. And he sat down, and taught the people out of the ship.*
> *4 Now when he had left speaking, he said unto Simon, Launch out into the deep, and let down your nets for a draught.*
> *5 And Simon answering said unto him, Master, we have toiled all the night, and have taken nothing: nevertheless at thy word I will let down the net.*
> *6 And when they had this done, they enclosed a great multitude of fishes: and their net brake.*
> *7 And they beckoned unto their partners, which were in the other ship, that they should come and help them. And they came, and filled both the ships, so that they began to sink.*

Peter and his fishing crew had fished all night long and caught absolutely nothing. Imagine their chagrin. Certainly they were depressed, based on the futility of their effort. When they encountered Jesus, He instructed them to go back and try again. Only, this time they were to cast their net out even farther. Of course, they begin to explain the circumstances that surrounded their current futility. "We have fished all night and caught nothing," they told Jesus. I'm sure there was a bit of arrogance on display, since they were expert fisherman. Why go back now when it's not conducive to catching anything. Of course, by this time of morning, the fish would be able to see their shadows. This makes no sense, they must have thought. In spite of being highly influenced by their emotions, they obeyed Jesus based on their faith, and not their emotions and anxieties. Believe it or not, sometimes your faith has to co-exist with your anxieties.

In spite of Jesus telling them to cast their *nets* into the deep, it appears they decided to cast only one *net.* Their anxieties affected their faith but did not negate it. Being that this did not make a lot of sense to them, there was no need in casting out all of the nets they had just cleaned, so they simply cast out one net. Though they would not be foolish enough to disobey Jesus, they did not completely comply with his demand. Their anxieties effected their total compliance. However, their faith was illustrated by the fact that they were obedient and cast out into the deep waters.

Their catch overwhelmed their net, and though much was caught, much was lost, because they did not comply completely. Still their faith had to co-exist with their anxieties, and their faith prevailed. Though it made no sense intellectually, and though they initially balked at the demand of Jesus, faith manifested will always bring its just reward. They had more fish than they could handle. *Thank you Pastor Twymon,* I couldn't leave it out.

As Christians, we are constantly overcoming fears or wrestling with emotions that challenge our faith. It is a very difficult task sometimes to handle the volatile mix of emotions and faith. If we are not careful, everything we believe appears to blow up in our faces when circumstances around us leave us hapless and forlorn. This is when you need to know that your faith, (*your response to God based on your trust*) will triumph over your anxieties, because God is in control.

My oldest daughter, Jaketta, has had her share of problems with childbirth. She has had four miscarriages, though, she and her husband James, have been blessed with three beautiful children. While every one of my grandchildren is a divine blessing to me, the birth of the last one, Jaia (pronounced Jay-Ah) which means, VICTORY, was a revelation to me as far as fear and faith having to coexist. Jaketta was not due to give birth to Jaia until approximately February 21, 2010. However, God had another plan. God designed that she would be born November 11th 2009, 14 weeks ahead of time, and it caused a lot of anxiety and fear.

It was November 11th 2009 when I received the call that the baby was coming now, ready or not. I jumped into my car and sped to the hospital. Man, did I have a lot of thoughts on the way to the hospital! As I prayed for my daughter and my new grandbaby, I simply asked God for what I wanted...*a miracle*. I also asked Him to help us all accept whatever His will was going to be.

In spite of the faith that I know I have in God, I was scared to death as I rushed to the hospital. I was thinking of all of the scenarios that the doctors had painted for us if this pregnancy did not go full term, or at least 28 weeks. I was afraid for my child and my grandbaby. I was not shaking with fear, but I was truly apprehensive.

Now there are many who would say I did not have a genuine faith in God, or I would not have been afraid. To that I would say *"bah humbug,"* not true. I know that I have a true and active faith in God. However, the domicile (residence) of my faith is a human body, which is a very frail container in which to hold spiritual things. This container is often subject to fear when overwhelmed with circumstances that are far beyond its control. I thought at best Jaia had a 50-50 chance, and that's not very encouraging when your life is on the line.

Without question, fear can be a detriment to our faith, but it's only fatal when it hinders us from responding to God with a trusting disposition, but not simply because you are afraid. It's not that I am never anxious, but I am never paralyzed by my fear to the extent that I will not trust God and what He says to me.

Though I *wrestled* with my fear, I *rested* on my faith, and I cried out to the true and living God, who hears the cries of His children. Because God hears, He answers. We don't always get the answer we want but at least we can lay it at His feet. What a joy and relief to know that we are never alone in our times of travail.

It was my faith in God that made me respond to what the Bible teaches about God, and I had confidence that He would give me strength to endure His answer even if it was not congruent to my request. I also know, by faith, that He will give you some of the desires of your heart. This was one of those times in my life when my fear co-existed with my faith, yet my faith was genuine.

Well, my grandbaby Jaia came in weighing only 1 lb, 13 ounces. She was in a very precarious situation, but she came with a heart to fight. As of this date, February 1, 2010 she weighs 5lbs and is due to come home by Friday February 5, 2010. She is breathing on her own, and she is known at the hospital as the *"overweight pre-mee."*

As we continue to pray for her, we thank God for the grace He has granted once again. Because faith has everything to do with what we cannot see and understand, anxiety is often an unwelcome companion but not an overpowering foe…by keeping us from responding to God with confidence and praise.

Your faith is best exhibited when you obey God. Obedience is the only response that illustrates that your faith is genuine. Though I was afraid for my grandbaby, I was not going to allow my fear to make me forget how good God has been to my family.

In the Gospel of Mark 4:35-41, we are told the story of the disciples being suddenly caught in the middle of an unsuspecting storm while Jesus rested calmly in the bottom of the boat. The boat was being tossed violently back and forth by the wind and the waves. The boat had begun to take on water, and it seemed that sinking was inevitable. The disciples feared for their lives and beseeched Jesus to save them. They actually asked Him whether he cared or not about the possibility of them perishing because death certainly seemed eminent. These professional fishermen were literally frightened out of their minds..

Scripture informs us that Jesus arose from His slumber, came up from the bottom of the boat, rebuked the wind and the waves, demanded calm, and the storm ceased. As we bask in the power and authority of our Lord and Savior Jesus Christ, we must never lose sight of the fact that Jesus is always concerned with our welfare, no matter how perilous the times may be.

These disciples have often been criticized and scorned for their fear, as if they had no right to be afraid. Who of us would not have been afraid in such a dire situation as this? I have been saturated with fear in circumstances that were less life threatening. Though Jesus admonished them for the magnitude of their fear, (verse 40) it must be understood in light of the context that is availed to us. It was not a mandate to never be afraid of anything.

Let's go back to the beginning of the chapter and get further insight. The disciples had been with Jesus throughout the day as he went about teaching in regards to the kingdom of God. In the past, they had been witnesses to His miracles; therefore they knew of His power. Jesus taught about the Parable Of The Sower, The Lamp On A Stand, The Parable Of The Growing Seed, and The Parable Of The Mustard Seed, leading up to the storm. The 4th Chapter of Mark informs us that Jesus met privately with them to share secret things.

In Mark 4:9 Jesus says to them, "he who has ears to hear let him hear." In other words be a willing listener to the words of God. *Listen carefully, because* you may miss something very important. Pay attention to the words of God. Don't get distracted by things that don't matter.

In the present scenario surrounding the storm, Jesus appears to admonish them quite harshly, when you consider the severity of the storm. I asked myself, who wouldn't have been afraid in a situation like this? Jesus, however, admonishes them in light of all that had gone on around them. Didn't they realize who was with them in the midst of this storm? Did they not understand whom they belonged to and what authority He had?

On top of all of this, they had not listened carefully. Just prior to embarking on the journey across the lake,

Jesus had actually informed them of the outcome of their journey. In verse 35 Jesus said, *"Let's go over to the other side."* Had they been listening carefully, they would have remembered that Jesus declared that they were going over to the other side. This clearly implied that we ARE going to make it to the other side, no matter what we may encounter. Therefore, why are you so afraid of the storm when I have already stated the conclusion of our journey at the beginning of it?

Jesus admonished them for their degree of fear because they had not paid attention. Had they listened carefully and paid attention to what had been going on around them, they would have known that they were going to make it. It's not that people of faith are never afraid, but they are never afraid to the degree that they are blind to the sovereignty and power of God.

Don't wait to overcome your fears or anxieties before you respond to God in a positive way. Trust is not something you have to feel; it's something you have to illustrate. Even when you don't understand, faith will still prevail if you respond to God with a trusting spirit---even when you're overcome with fear.

When My Anxieties Wrestle With My Faith

Life has its way of taking you
Where you may not choose to go.
Faith calls on you to still believe
God is in control.

The lines of worry have left their trace
Faith calls you to endure.
You're blessed to be in God's embrace
His wisdom to procure.

Fear desires to break your spirit
That lies so deep within.
Faith tells you that God's not finished
Hold on until the end.

Oft times we choose to deny our fears,
For it threatens who we are.
Quite possibly behind our tears
Lie unrepentant scars.

My faith is real in spite of
Some fears I entertain.
It's God who puts my soul at ease,
For His purpose is germane.

"Joy cometh in the morning," says He.
"I'll make all wrong things right.
Drive fear away with spurning, trust Me.
I will see you through the night."

So though you may be anxious,
Don't give into your fears.
Stand on your faith regardless
And know your prayer, He hears.

By Jake Gaines Jr.

Chapter 4

Doing My Faith With Determination

Faith can move mountains, but don't be surprised if God hands you a shovel-- Author Unknown

One of the most difficult aspects of faith is allowing it to manifest itself in our lives on a consistent basis. We are very comfortable talking about it, yet apprehensive when it comes to it being on display. Our faith should constantly be on display like a mannequin in a department store window, visible for all to see. Nothing glorifies God more than displaying His presence in our life...through our life.

When I say we need to be *doing our faith*, I mean that we should be actively portraying the trust we have in Christ by following Him. The more we portray Christ, the more visible Christ becomes to the world around us. Doing our faith with determination simply requires us to put ourselves on *"display"* for others to see how serious we are about our relationship and love for Jesus Christ.

Our faith is not something that we have to feel emotionally, but rather, a determination to do things God's way due to the trust and belief we have in Him. *This faith is being driven by what we believe but cannot see, and fortified by what we see and cannot believe.* God has done enough unbelievable things in MY life for me to trust Him and forge my way through difficult times, regardless of how I feel about them. Our faith ought to be seen clearly enough for us to literally be defined by it. We should be so closely associated with our faith through our actions that people cannot define us except through our trust in God.

We should be known for our divine determination. We should be remembered for our tenacity in Christ, in spite of what our obstacles may be. Even if we do not stand out intellectually, we should stand tall in our determination to live for Christ, as others see us fight diligently to draw near to Him for strength and healing. If ever a faith was defined by its determination, it was the biblical story of the lady with an issue of blood.

Mark 5:25-34

> *A large crowd followed and pressed around him. [25]And a woman was there who had been subject to bleeding for twelve years. [26]She had suffered a great deal under the care of many doctors and had spent all she had, yet instead of getting better she grew worse. [27]When she heard about Jesus, she came up behind him in the crowd and touched his cloak, [28]because she thought, "If I just touch his clothes, I will be healed." [29]Immediately her bleeding stopped and she felt in her body that she was freed from her suffering. [30]At once Jesus realized that power had gone out from him. He turned around in the crowd and asked, "Who touched my clothes?" [31]"You see the people crowding against you," his disciples answered, "and yet you can ask, 'Who touched me?' "[32]But Jesus kept looking around to see who had done it. [33]Then the woman, knowing what had happened to her, came and fell at his feet and, trembling with fear, told him the whole truth. [34]He said to her, "Daughter, your faith has healed you. Go in peace and be freed from your suffering."*

This was a woman who had already exercised an enormous amount of faith by seeking one physician after another, looking for a cure to her affliction. For at least twelve years she had sought help and had spent all of her money doing so. It's obvious that she at least believed she could be healed by her relentless pursuit of a knowledgeable doctor.

Her faith (in physicians) had been displayed for all to see. In spite of all of her efforts, she had found no cure after twelve years, yet she was undaunted by her plight and relentless in her pursuit of a healing. This woman truly symbolized being a *doer* of her faith, no matter what.

Doing your faith with determination is an active response to what you believe. She believed she could find a doctor that could heal her, yet she did not. However, she was one who manifested her faith in a genuine effort of her own. She was accustomed to acting out her faith. Now that her faith was properly directed toward the right object, which was Jesus, she simply did what she was used to doing, actively responding to what she believed to be true.

The woman began to work her way toward Jesus to secure her healing. There is a particular indication that this woman was of the Jewish faith. If you notice, her initial intent was just to touch the hem of His garment for her healing. It appears that she was quite aware of the fact that she would cause Jesus to be ceremonially unclean by touching His body, due to the fact that she was bleeding.

What this woman would have to endure, just to get to Jesus, would have likely discouraged the most staunched believer. The public ridicule alone would have been demeaning enough to thwart most efforts. In spite of this, she pressed on toward Jesus with the faith that she had. This faith in Jesus may have been forced upon her through necessity. She may have felt that she was out of options, and it was time to turn to Jesus. Whatever the case may be, an active faith will not be unrewarded. It is not so much our attitude about our faith as it is being solely driven by it. What is truly encouraging is, it does not matter why you won't give up on your faith, just as long as you don't. Your response to your faith may sometimes be fueled by fear, anger, frustration, or any variety of emotions. God's response to your faith is determined by your active response to His will and His ways, not your feelings.

This woman's actions spoke loudly of how she believed Jesus could and would heal her based on what she had heard and/or knew of Him and His ministry. The point is, she was now convinced that Jesus was the answer, and she was not going to let anything or anybody hinder her from being in His presence.

Those of us who, as the apostle Paul stated, are "persuaded" (convinced) that Jesus Christ is the answer to life's purpose and eternity's glory, should not let anything hinder us from being in His presence through prayer and meditation. If our faith, in fact, is genuine, it must be manifested in our visible efforts.

This woman pressed on, though most likely she was in a weakened state from the constant loss of blood. She pressed on because she believed, and she believed because she heard, and through hearing, she was convinced she could be healed. She pressed through the throng of people that would have caused the faint of heart to give up at the very beginning.

Though this woman was convinced that Jesus had the power to heal her, she apparently had some reservations about how he might respond to her. It seems that she was not thoroughly convinced that Jesus would show her mercy. Therefore, she entertained the thought of just sneaking up behind Him and touching His garment to procure a healing from His clothing alone. This clearly shows that you do not have to have the greatest of confidence that God is willing to do something for the grace of God to be extended to you. You must however, believe that He can extend His grace and present yourself to Him in whatever state you find yourself.

So often we try to get things right before we genuinely surrender ourselves to God. Many believe that they have to quit drinking, cursing, gambling, using drugs, fornicating, or any other form of sin before they can receive the mercy of God. They will not come before Him until they quit bleeding. They must first seek other options. This is a painful and costly mistake. This woman tried everything she knew, with no favorable results before she turned to Jesus. She may have made Jesus her last option out of ignorance of His person and ministry, or it could have just been stubbornness. Most likely she had run out of money. In any case, she was now pressing her way toward the Master, not to be deterred.

Faith is not something you have to master, but it is something you have to manifest. It's amazing to me how much we attempt to do to *get faith* when we simply need to persevere *in faith.* How about just not giving up on the faith you already have? Certainly the allure of something new has great drawing power. Just the mere thought of **NEW** generates excitement in us.

I remember my first 3 years of playing golf. Man, was I excited about every new type of golf club I could get my hands on! From $90.00 putters to $300.00 drivers ($1000.00 today) *No! I do not have one.* Oh, what great promises of golf excellence spilled out from every TV commercial! "This is the club you need. No! This is the club you need, NOOOO! This is what you need to be a better golfer." I love to play golf, however, in spite of all the new equipment I bought in those first 3 years of playing, I'm still not very good at it after playing for 7 years.

The reality of this was I had not developed a good golf swing with the old clubs that I already owned; therefore I was simply applying a bad swing onto some brand new clubs. Tearfully, my game did not improve. (Do you understand my point?) This reminds me of when Jesus told the Pharisees of the uselessness *of "putting old wine into new bottles."* Quite frankly, I needed to persevere in lessons and practice, or it would not matter what type of clubs I owned. We must first learn to persevere in the faith that we already have, or we will simply put a bad swing on any new level of faith we may obtain.

It is not necessary that you feel great about your faith but that you never stop persevering in it. Don't give up on trusting God. When it seems that you are on the precipice of giving up on your faith, ask yourself, what or whom you are giving up your blessing for.? Do you gain more by giving up on God, or do you lose more? It is your decision, but at least seek wise council. Don't allow the blind to lead the blind.

The woman pressed on toward Jesus. Although there were many obstacles to overcome, she did her part and pressed on. She did her faith with determination. Galatians 6:9 tells us: *don't grow weary in well doing, for you shall reap in due season, if you do not faint.* Do not quit on your faith. Pressing on toward the presence of Jesus is the right thing to do, and we must never grow tired of doing what's right.

Once she fights through all of the obstacles to get to Jesus, something very interesting occurs. In the midst of all the people, Jesus recognizes that He has been touched by someone. He recognized that power had gone from Him. This prompted Jesus to ask, "Who touched my clothes?" The disciples were mystified by the question that seemed to make no sense at all, being that the crowd was so large and dense that everyone was bumping into each other. It was literally impossible *not* to be touched.

In my opinion, this is one of the most intriguing miracles of healing in the Bible because it is so very different from many of the others. This woman was actually trying to sneak up on Jesus just to touch His garment. There was a common belief of that day, that by touching holy men of God or the garments they wore, it could often result in a miracle. She intended to touch His garment in the midst of the crowd and then scurry on her way.

Jesus was not paying any attention to her, nor did He have any special compassion for her in particular because He did not acknowledge her beforehand. It's safe to assume that he did not even see her. As misled as the woman's faith was, it was genuine and *Christ directed*, therefore it resulted in her being healed.

The quality of your faith is more determined by what it will make you do and endure as opposed to how much you think you have. Ask yourself how you would determine the amount of faith that you have? Do you measure it with a yard stick, or weigh it, or does it make more sense to acknowledge your determination in it? With what degree of tenacity do you respond to your faith? This woman responded with a determination that bellowed that her faith was of great quality.

This woman had a specific purpose… to see Jesus. She was not there because she was just following the crowd. She was not there to see any other person. She was not there just for religious reasons. She was there to be healed, and she believed Jesus could do it, and she was not going to be turned away because of any Jewish laws and traditions that forbade her from seeing Jesus. This was not about religion. This was about her being in the presence of Jesus and receiving a healing.

So often we let the opinion of others keep us away from the presence of Jesus. We simply stop going to church, Bible study, or reading our Bible. We ultimately take whatever faith we have and direct it toward something or someone else that cannot provide us with a healing. We then become discouraged and ultimately give up on our faith. In essence, we foil our own faith by changing our direction, thus altering the object of our faith. When we lose confidence in God, we lose our spiritual determination also. We just don't have the zeal to fight for what is rightfully ours, in spite of what the Word of God may tell us. We allow our circumstances to drown out the voice of God.

The woman was healed initially, without Jesus even knowing who she was. It was not until afterwards that she was identified. Jesus, not wanting her to leave with the belief that she had magically received a healing, informs her that she received her healing through a divine formula. *Faith + Jesus = Healing.* Through His Word, Jesus wants us to know that the power came from Him and not through some mystical exercise. It culminated through her faith, which fanned the flame of her determination.

"Daughter, your faith has healed you," Jesus said to her. Your faith, as illustrated by the way you responded, resulted in your healing. You would not give up despite the obstacles that you faced. You pressed on in spite of your loss of blood and being declared unclean. You fought through ridicule and prejudices, and you directed your faith toward me.

She was healed because her faith was the driving force that propelled her to the source of her healing. This woman did not talk about her faith or brag about her faith; she *did her faith with determination*. She withstood the forces that rose up against her. She did what was necessary to promote a healing. She trusted in Jesus.

Are you willing to do your faith with determination and put it on display for all to see and scrutinize no matter what the circumstances may be? Are you willing to rise up against the obstacles that prohibit you from doing what you believe? I can't say that I have always been busy doing my faith with determination as much as I have tried to examine it. I realize now that doing my faith is the ultimate sign that my faith is genuine. No matter how feeble your faith may be at this point in your life, make a new commitment to start doing your faith no matter what. Do what you believe and receive the healings you are entitled to through our Lord and Savior Jesus Christ.

What a joy to see your faith rewarded at whatever level it may be. The most important element is, to *do your faith*. Let your *actions* reflect the belief that you have in your Lord and Savior, Jesus Christ.

Doing Your Faith

Do your faith each day you live
Live to do your faith each day
Let others see how much you give
As you go about your way

Though some may scoff at your love
When you stand strong and unfazed
Though you are spoken evil of
Let them stand, amazed

At how you always overcome
The obstacles you face
Not understanding what you know
About God's amazing grace

So, rely on what God says to you
Your resolve will oft be tested
Your faith is seen in what you do
So God's glory is manifested.

By Jake Gaines Jr.

Chapter 5

When My Practical Living
Catches Up To My Cognitive Faith

Faith isn't the ability to believe long and far into the misty future. It's simply taking God at His Word and taking the next step.

- Joni Erickson Tada

We all became Christians through our faith in Jesus Christ as our Lord and Savior. We made a conscious decision to give our lives to Him based on believing that He died on the cross for our sins. We believe that He was buried and on the third day He arose by the power of the Holy Spirit with all the authority in heaven and on earth. This allowed us to be reconciled to God. Upon accepting Jesus as our savior, a major event occurred. Our position, as it related to our relationship with God, immediately changed. We ceased to be His enemies and became His children. We went from sinner to saint, from lost to found, from darkness to light, from His creation to His personal possession. All of our sins (transgressions against God) have been forgiven, and we are now new creatures in Christ.

All of this and more occurred in the twinkling of an eye, and without any input from us, simply through the grace of God because of His great love for us. We became filled with power from the Holy Spirit, which now dwells within us and gives us the power to live a transformed life pleasing to God by directing us and empowering us to embrace the ways of God. What a wonderful and exciting experience. What a loving gesture from the Almighty God.

In spite of this awesome experience through the love of God, there still exists an enigma that cannot be ignored. We see that many Christians, myself included, found that it was an enormous struggle to live this newly created life on a consistent basis. I found, like Peter, that my love for God alone would not keep me from grieving Him with the sins in my life. We still struggle with the flesh and its enticing draw.

In spite of our faith (trust) in God, we find that our everyday living consistently lags behind the trust that we feel we have. It just seems that no matter how hard we try, our lives don't seem to measure up to the faith we declare we have. This may be because we see faith as some magic potion that makes our lives what God wants them to be in one single *poof.* In spite of our declaration of love and faithfulness, we wrestle with, and many times, succumb to the ways and temptations of the flesh. How can this be when you know in your heart of hearts that you do love God and trust in Him?

We must embrace the fact that we must make a concerted effort to do things God's way. We must decide to work at the things that align our lives with the will of God. We must study His word arduously. We must pray fervently for the will of God in our lives. We must bask in venues that allow us to give ourselves to others willingly. We must surrender ourselves to God's plan in our lives and trust the results.

We have a responsibility to work hard so that our lives line up with what we believe. I know you have to believe something first before you can truly submit to it, but once you believe, you must then work feverishly through the power of the Holy Spirit to line your life up with your belief. This is what I mean by *"your living catching up to your faith."* Just having that faith without a plan or objective to make that faith manifest in your life is just ecclesiastical folly.

Having faith in God is also knowing and trusting that God's grace is sufficient through the difficulties of your growth period and that it can vary from one Christian to another. This does not give you a license to sin against God whenever you choose. Rather, it is an incomparable act of love by God, to be merciful, and it should be revered and not taken for granted.

Romans 6:1-4

> *¹What shall we say, then? Shall we go on sinning so that grace may increase? ²By no means! We died to sin; how can we live in it any longer? ³Or don't you know that all of us who were baptized into Christ Jesus were baptized into his death? ⁴We were therefore buried with him through baptism into death in order that, just as Christ was raised from the dead through the glory of the Father, we too may live a new life.*

God's grace should draw us even closer to Him with a more contrite spirit as we recognize His great mercy toward us. This act of grace should make us even more committed to God as He protects us and guides us through this tedious process of maturity. Since there is such a great disparity between our character and God's character, there can often be a major gap between our living on a daily basis and our faith in God. Though this is not to be taken lightly in any way, it also should not be looked upon as a hapless situation in which God does not care. We simply must surrender more of ourselves to God and let Him complete His work in us.

Having faith in God is more than just trusting Him to be who He says He is and to do what He says He will do. It is a faith that believes and trusts that, in spite of all of our flaws, God will still finish His work in us and that we are required to continue to trust Him. Despite what many of us believe, we do not have the option to just give up on God's methods, no matter how perplexing they may be. Many of us believe that we can just opt out of commitment to God whenever it is convenient. Instead, we must kneel before the authority of God with fear and trembling, recognizing his sovereignty (complete control) and we must bask in it.

Contrary to the popular belief that the responsibility to grow spiritually is all on God, we need to understand that we have a responsibility to work, and work, and work until our everyday living catches up with our professed trust in God. I am in total agreement that the more you trust God, the more righteous your living will become. Yet in spite of this fact, it is very important that you understand that the more you trust God in your living, the more productive your spiritual life will become, and this is the visual proof that God is working in you. I always tell my congregants that *"Salvation is free, spiritual growth is not."*

So many Christians believe, in theory, that God's way is the best way, but they often do not experience in their lives what they believe in their mind. This is commonly the result of them not applying God's Word consistently to their lives.

These are people who refuse to endure the struggle of allowing their living to catch up with their faith. We refuse to recognize that we have a lot of work to do. We want God to do all of the work while we simply wait for better results. James 1:22 tell us, *"Do not merely listen to the word, and so deceive yourselves. Do what it says."* Simply put, "live what you believe." Trust God enough to put your belief into action. This is the visible manifestation of the work of God.

This process often takes longer than we would like, but this is where true faith comes into play. How faithful will you be to God when you are not experiencing the results you would like in your Christian walk? It is *"not seeing"* and yet continuing to work hard to live a holy and righteous life. This is the very foundation of what faith is. The Bible tells us that if you can see it, then it is not faith. Sometimes we cannot see what God is doing in us, but we are obligated as His children to strive with great vigor to live for Christ. Even without seeing immediate progress in your own growth in spite of your trust in God, you must strive to incorporate the ways of God into your life. God will reward your obedience regardless of how you feel about your situation. God does not bless us based on our feelings; rather He honors His Word, which will result in our blessings. Your living will catch up with your faith when you simply *"do what God says to do."* Your everyday life will begin to reflect the righteousness of God.

The Apostle Peter is an excellent example of a person who loved God and was a faithful follower of Jesus Christ. Yet he struggled mightily in many areas of his spiritual life. Peter was a true enigma. He was a raw, unrefined fisherman called to be an apostle of Christ. I don't think there is any question that Peter was a man who loved Jesus Christ. He left everything he had and all that he held dear to him to become a disciple of Christ.

Peter trusted Jesus and His ministry. He believed Jesus was the Son of God and the Messiah that had been prophesied about in the scriptures, who would come and save sinners from eternal destruction. Despite these beliefs, Peter struggled mightily at times to translate that faith into his everyday living. This was in part because Peter believed that his faith in, and love for, Christ alone would always translate into the proper behavior.

Despite Peter's love for Jesus, he denied Christ for fear of being exposed as a disciple and losing his life. Peter often felt his love alone for Jesus would sustain him in his living. Yet, just as Jesus predicted, before the cock crowed, he denied Him three times. When Peter should have been praying, he slept. He believed his love for Jesus alone was enough to sustain him. It was not. Peter should have been working through prayer. We too, find ourselves sleeping when we should pay attention to the small details of life that warn us of how frail and fragile we are when it comes to the process of growing in Christ. When you look at Peter in the Gospels and then compare him to the Peter in the epistles 1st and 2nd Peter, you have to wonder if it's the same man. It is… some thirty years later and we can see the results of his living catching up to his profession of faith.

For your living to catch up with your faith, you must have a desire to change and to do the things necessary to get to higher plateaus of spirituality. Though your faith may be sincere, your efforts to change must become a greater priority in your life. You have to surround yourself with different resources if you want to grow in Christ. You also have to understand that not everyone will be able to go with you through certain trials and tests. You must be willing to grow alone sometimes. We may not like it, but it's often necessary so that we are not distracted.

Our living (daily practical living) will begin to catch up with our professed faith when we make a cognitive decision and effort to change. It happens when we take on the responsibility of a disciple of Christ and go through the necessary process to be more like Christ. The visible manifestation of God working within us is our decision to let Christ in our hearts (the deepest part of our thinking) with the intent of following and not leading.

Just because you flounder in your Christian walk does not mean God is not at work in you any longer, rather it's more that you may not be taking your part in this relationship seriously enough to *endure the hardships of growth*. This not only stunts your growth but also affects others who watch to see what God is doing in your life.

It is crucial that you understand that your Christian walk does not just affect you. Others are influenced by the way you live your life as a child of God. Since we do not live our lives in a vacuum, the way we walk in the *light* of Jesus Christ, can implicate others. We must work diligently, if our practical living is to catch up to our cognitive belief. What we think about God will only show up in our everyday living if we work at it. Don't just sit around doubting your faith, put in the effort to have it manifest itself in your life. The more you test your faith, the stronger it will become, and ultimately your confidence in God will increase as you consult Him more in your decision making.

Living for Christ is more than showing up for church functions and giving your financial support. As crucial as these elements are, they are just a part of our responsibility as people of God. If you truly believe in the bowels of your mind that God is the answer to your life, you must step up your efforts to be an example of what believing in Jesus Christ is all about. So many Christians believe that God just wants their participation in a religious setting and not possession of their lives. He wants all of us. He wants our souls, our bodies, and our minds.

Visit your Pastor sometimes, and ask him to help you recognize the things you need to do, to better manifest the actual living of your cognitive belief. You need to step out of the box that has held you captive for so many years and dare to encounter new experiences in your Christian walk. God is a progressive God. He does not want you to stagnate, but to trust Him to take you where you need to be in your Christian growth.

The time is now for us to illustrate the Christ like behavior that we have failed to show in the past. Give of yourself in a way that you have never given before. Make yourself more available. Open yourself up to the needs of others, even if it puts you in a position of vulnerability. Challenge yourself to seek out spiritual venues that you once thought to be beyond your reach. These are just suggestions to encourage you to live your faith. *This may be a challenge for you right now, but God will give you* **comfort** *in your trial, though you might be* **comfortable.**

If you know you believe and trust in God, you must then live out what you believe if you want to experience the Christian growth that leaves you wholesome and fulfilled. Start trusting God in a new way today. Get busy with the task of allowing others to see God working in you in a special way. You may be the lifeline of someone else who has lost hope in experiencing the new life of a new creation.

Living
What I Believe

Living what I believe
What a challenge who could
know?
How hard it is to receive
The challenges to grow

To show the change God's
made in me
Others to encourage
How His grace has set me free
As He rids me of the baggage

That sin had put upon me
And saddled me with guilt
Jesus gave his life for me
That mine could be rebuilt

So, I live to give Him glory
I strive to praise His name
I commit to live the story
And righteously acclaim

That Jesus is the answer
To my futility
And dare I do not barter
With God's sovereignty

I have nothing to offer
Only to receive
From this loving Anchor
It is Him, to whom I cleave

So I do my faith,
not speak of it
It's easier to see
A faith that's manifested
Has this effect, on me

It leaves me energetic
In most challenging of times
It silences my critics
It is the tie that binds

And when I think it's useless
To stand and be my faith
God's love just leaves me
breathless
As I wallow in His grace.

By Jake Gaines Jr.

Chapter 6

Focusing My Faith

To one who has faith, no explanation is necessary.
To one without faith no explanation is possible---
Thomas Aquinas

Throughout my Christian journey, I have never heard a word taught, preached, or simply mentioned as often as the word faith. The Bible tells us that we receive our salvation through faith.

Romans 5:1

> *Therefore, since we have been justified through faith, we[a] have peace with God through our Lord Jesus Christ, [2]through whom we have gained access by faith into this grace in which we now stand.*

Faith is, without question the linchpin between us and God. It is what separates us from non-believers, who cannot experience true conviction in the soul. They cannot bring themselves to believe in someone without visible proof of their existence. Faith is what assures us that we are going to be fine, simply because God says so.

What is it about faith that causes us to struggle with it being active and visible in our everyday lives? We willingly concede the fact that it is a necessity for our spiritual survival. It is clearly something we enjoy talking about and yet, it is one of the greatest perplexities with which a Christian must deal. Why do we struggle so much trusting God?

One reason in particular that comes to mind very quickly for me is the fact that we spend an enormous amount of time fighting against the ways of God and I'm not sure if we are consciously aware of it. We simply do this by doing things *our way* and not His. It is not open defiance, but a subtle disconnection orchestrated by Satan. By doing things our way we unintentionally tell God that His way does not work consistently enough for us to trust on an everyday basis.

This mindset chips away at the foundation of our faith. As a result, material things and situations that have no long-term affect on our spiritual growth, become distractions to us. If we cannot trust God, we (mankind) are the only ones left to trust, and that is the end of our spiritual growth.

Trust is the key word here because that is what faith is all about. We must trust that God is who He says He is and live our lives based on that trust. We must not only believe in His existence but also His work. We must know that everything He does is for our greatest benefit no matter how difficult it is to humanly comprehend. We must believe more than just the historicity of Christ. By this, I mean your belief in Jesus Christ must go beyond the historical facts that He came, He lived, and He died for our sins. Many believe the historical facts about Jesus, but they cannot truly believe that what He accomplished in His sacrificial death was enough to make us right with the Father. We MUST believe that Jesus' death on the cross and His resurrection from the grave are all we need to have a relationship with God and to live our lives based on that belief in our Lord and Savior Jesus Christ. Anything short of this is generic, and it simply WILL NOT suffice.

I believe that one of the main reasons we struggle in the area of our faith is that we see faith as something that we gather up and accumulate over a certain period of time or through specific types of experiences. It's as if we believe that once we get to a certain level of faith, we will reach this spiritual quota that will catapult us beyond the reach of life's negative circumstances. This belief blinds us to the fact that faith is not something we feel, but something we must prove through our living.

It is no mystery as to why so many people who gather in our churches on Sunday mornings are still fragmented and confused about their relationship with God. These people work so hard to gain God's favor, as if Jesus has not provided all that is necessary to secure our relationship. Unfortunately, they believe that with harder work and better attendance they somehow will stockpile enough faith to be what God wants them to be. They never reach that point because their understanding of faith is erroneous.

Clearly, faith is not defined by how you feel about it, but instead by how you demonstrate it in your life. It is a faith that is so clearly defined by its focus on God that your humility is never in question. Everything you do is for God to get the glory.

You do not have to feel like being obedient, you simply do what is pleasing to God because of your faith that God will justly reward you for your allegiance to Him. I have often wondered why our declaration of faith does not translate into a different and bolder behavior in our everyday lives.

It is apparent to me that some Christians believe that faith is somehow duty-bound to eliminate the possibility of failure. The truth of the matter is, if the possibility of failure did not exist, faith would not be necessary. The very fact that faith does not negate the possibility of failure is the driving force that makes us plow through our fears and trust that God has a victory for us on the other side of our efforts. It is about being active because of the assurance that God will allow our efforts to produce fruitful results.

One of the most telling characteristics of faith is that you do not need a mountain of confidence to get started with anything that God has revealed for you to do. I love a statement that I heard Charles Stanley say, which was, *"Obey God, and leave the consequences to Him."* You are trusting that God will manifest Himself through you in such a way that it will defy the natural order of things. You simply step out on faith and obey the mandate of God. We must understand that the possibility of us failing is always before us, yet always behind God.

Because faith challenges us to step out of our comfort zone, we have a tendency to look for additional confirmation from outside sources, looking for something or someone else to assure us that we are doing the right thing at the right time. Faith does not require confirmation from other people. Faith IS the confirmation, and all it requires is *action.*

Have you ever noticed how we are always praying for more, more, and more of something? We don't ever seem to have enough.   It's no different with our faith. WE WANT MORE!!! Tell me this, why should God give us more of anything to do less with, especially for Him? Do you really need more of what you are not effectively and efficiently using? I would think "<u>NOT!!!!</u>".

When the object (focus) of your faith is God, it will generate a response directly correlated to your belief that

God will honor His end of the bargain, no matter how difficult the task may be. The results of the task are certainly influenced by your ability to get the job done; however, the ultimate results are based on trusting in the power of God.

With this in mind, a person can begin a task that seems to be virtually impossible to accomplish through his or her own ability. Faith, properly directed, would divert the focus from the one who is attempting a task to the one who is demanding the task to be done. A focused faith ignites in us a desire to get busy with the task at hand and paralyzes the fear that would hold us back.

Earlier we discussed the woman with the issue of blood who was determined to get to Jesus for her healing. The focus there was her determination and actions (doing her faith). Now we want to make sure that whatever faith you have is directed at the one who can make a difference. *Who is your faith directed toward?*

We operate through the concept of faith all the time without even thinking about it. We sit down in chairs that we never check beforehand for safety purposes because we have sat in them before, and we have faith that they will hold us. How much faith you had was not the key factor, but instead it was the object of your faith (the chair) which you trusted that made you respond the way you did. Your faith was in the *chair.*

In spite of the fact that God has never failed us, and we do not question His *power,* we often doubt His *willingness* to do for us. When we doubt God's willingness to respond to us, we have the tendency to try to fix things ourselves, in spite of our miserable record of failure. *I know I am truly guilty of this.* Our faith must be focused to such an extent that it is like a racehorse with blinders on, oblivious to everything around him and focused solely on the finish line.

A focused faith never allows the failures of the past to influence the current decision at hand. A focused faith forgets the last set of circumstances, no matter how painful, and zeroes in on the one who has the ability to accomplish the task, which is God. Even when I have failed miserably, it was never because it was God's design for me to be a *failure*, but often because I did not do it His way and for His purpose.

A focused faith cannot hear the naysayers and the critics. It cannot succumb to doubts and fears, even though it may experience these negative emotions. A focused faith is so in tune with God that nothing around you matters. The circumstances do not matter. The timing does not matter. The people do not matter. The lack of resources does not matter. Nothing else matters because all you can see and hear is the one who is directing you in your endeavor and who has empowered you to accomplish it.

It often astounds me that we give so much credence to people who stand tall and bellow out as critics, about what you can and cannot do, and yet they have accomplished so very little themselves. Why do we give such credibility to people who try to discourage us, when we know what God has said to us? What makes other people's opinions and philosophies so important to us? Could it be that you have so little confidence in what you know and understand about God, that other people's viewpoints are more important? This can be rectified by personally studying the Word of God. You will then have the truth, and you can move forward with confidence.

One of the devil's most potent weapons is distraction. As subtle as it may be, it has the ability to be very destructive. Little subtle delays in what can be done now will rob you of your focus. Being around the wrong type of people, who constantly wrestle against your spirit, can rob you of your focus. You are not obligated to put up with people on a continuous basis, who live their lives opposite to yours. In the long-run these people will become constant distractions.

Your faith not only needs to be focused on the voice of God, but also onto His purpose, even when you don't know exactly what it is. God's purpose will not always be clear to us right away. With time and patience, God will manifest His purpose for our lives. We must however remain active in our pursuit of His ways. We also need to get involved in various ministries in your local church, because God will often reveal His purpose while we are serving in some capacity. *Remember, God generally shoots at a moving target.* Therefore, don't be one of those people who sit idly by waiting on clarity from God. To trust God is to trust His purpose, His method, His timing, and His results. It is the only way that we can truly immerse ourselves into the will of God. We have to give all of ourselves to Him, and we must believe that He will take us and mold us into what He wants us to be. What is your faith focused on? Are you focused on the task, or the God of the task?

When My Faith Is Focused

When my faith is focused
On Christ alone I find,
I'm able to accomplish
The things that are sublime.

As I immerse my will into His
Thrust into Holy action
I find so often that it is
The key to my distractions.

That life so readily submits
To turn my eyes away,
Determined as it never quits
Compelling me to sway,

Away from the thoughts of God
From the task at hand
It leads me to seek discord
Away from *The Master's* plan

Who's there to hold me firmly
In His holy grasp
Though my plight be dreary
I only need to ask

That God will keep me focused
On His will and on His way,
Safely I'm entrusted
To live a focused faith each day.

By Jake Gaines Jr.

Chapter 7

When My Faith Makes Me Weary

Belief is reassuring. People who live in the world of belief feel safe. On the contrary, faith is forever placing us on the razor's edge. ---Jacques Ellul

I know that my faith in God is genuine. There is no doubt in my mind that I truly trust God. In spite of this fact however, there are times when my faith in God is the very cause of my weariness in the flesh. As noted in the quote above, it is my faith that keeps me on the razor's edge.

We often find great comfort in our own little zone that we are so familiar with...thus the name "comfort zone"... brilliant, *right*? This little zone of familiarity is my greatest challenge because it gives me a false sense of control.

It is my faith in God that keeps me from trusting *myself* in spiritual things. It is that constant awareness that to trust myself will be detrimental to my spiritual growth. This constant wrestling match between "the things of God" and what my flesh desires can at times be so overwhelming that it simply wears me out.... physically, mentally and emotionally.

So many times I have no idea what God is doing in my life. Sometimes His methods can seem so contrary to mine that it's literally overwhelming. I struggle with defining moments (the true purpose) in my life. Spiritual clarity is a struggle from time to time. I struggle with God's timetable. I struggle with waiting. I struggle with His methods. I struggle with His demands. I struggle, sometimes, with His Word. Despite my struggles, I know that my deliverance is in trusting Him. One might ask, "How can you say you have faith in God and yet be wearied by your faith?"

Faith is not valid based on knowledge and logic. It is not always knowing, when, where, or how God is going to accomplish His purpose in you. Even the staunchest of Christians can struggle with waiting, while not knowing the outcome. It challenges your intellect, your patience, and your resolve, in spite of the fact that God has proven to you that He cannot fail.

Again, if you can see it, then it is not faith. If you already know the results, faith is not necessary. Therefore, you are always on the razor's edge...trusting what you cannot see, yet knowing in your heart that it's going to be OK. We are often unable to explain why we trust God so much and yet find ourselves anxious when our waiting begins to eat at us like vultures on a dead carcass.

My faith makes me weary sometimes because it is always challenging me to go beyond what I can see as a reality. That which I see, I can do. That does not cause me anxiety, but that which I know I am incapable of doing calls on all of my resolve toward faith. I must then trust God with all that I have within me. Despite the joy of knowing God will work things out, there is, sometimes, a weariness and a stressfulness that somehow I will find a way to get in the way of God and fail.

Faith wearies me on occasions because it requires me to pour myself into the will of God because I either don't know what to do or simply don't have the ability to get it done. As much as I teach and preach about faith, one would think that I would have a handle on how it works on an everyday basis. *Unfortunately, I don't always get it right either.* Again if I were right all the time, faith would never be necessary.

My faith requires me to be confident in what God is doing in my life while simultaneously leaving me to be openly battered by the opinions of on-lookers and others who don't have the faith I possess or simply do not know God like I do. Whether we want to admit it or not, this can become burdensome over a sustained period of time. There are times when I've wondered if I should wait and trust God in a particular situation or give in to my impatience and the need to know and just do it myself with the available resources. It seemed easier to let people think that I simply tried and failed than to go through the ridicule of others while they watched my periods of consternation as I waited on God, by trusting what I could not see.

Faith often wearies because it will not give in to circumstances. We should never get to a point where we do not consistently trust God because, *trusting God is what faith is.* Moreover, we must understand that our faith is always on the witness stand, being openly interrogated and laid out for all to see and evaluate.

Have you ever just wanted to have an old fashion "pity party" and wallow in your misery? You remember how you wanted to incorporate others into your "woe is me" smorgasbord to help reinforce your attitude? Can you remember how faith would join your party uninvited and challenge you to trust God? Faith reminded you that, while you could not see the light at the end of the tunnel, you needed to act like you knew it was there.

Of course this is, in part, an element of that spiritual warfare against the devil that is always attempting to get us to settle for less than we are entitled. No matter how we look at it, this vessel of clay (our bodies) that God has decided to use for His purpose and glory is flawed beyond our wildest imagination. It is only to the glory of God that He can use us at all.

My faith wearies me on occasion, yet I know that my faith has always and will always see me through. I wrestle with the guilt of not solely depending on it, when I know that it is my salvation. My faith constantly portrays a realistic view of myself and then renders me completely frustrated as to why I would even question the methods of God in the first place, as if I had a better idea (duh?).

My faith consistently reminds me that it is not governed by my comfort level, but instead, by what it is designed to do in achieving its objective, whatever that may be. The very faith that often wearies me in my flesh…. is my deliverer in my spirit, when my trials overwhelm me.

If your faith does not create challenges for you, then I doubt it is true faith at all. Faith is everything that logic is not. Faith requires us to not only believe in *things* that we cannot see, but to believe in SOMEONE that we cannot see.

Faith will not always bring us comfort as we define comfort. It will however, always bring us deliverance. God must honor His Word. If you trust Him (faith), He will deliver you from your trials. Your comfort may never be found in your circumstances, but rather in knowing that they will end in your deliverance. Sometimes, deliverance from trials is death. We may not find immediate comfort in that fact. On occasion, that deliverance you are anticipating may be rescuing you from you. Faith in God is more than trusting that God simply has *a* purpose for us. It is trusting that He has a *specific* purpose. Since we are already saved from the eternal penalty of sin, the faith that we live by is to help us surrender to the will of God. He pours our souls into His divine mold that He may shape us into His divine image.

When my faith wearies me, I know it's challenging me, and when it challenges me, I know it's active in me, and when it's active in me, I know that it is genuine.

Finally, I had to come to the realization that if my faith never wearies me, challenges me, or frustrates me, that it might not be faith at all. True faith won't allow me to arbitrarily take control of my decisions without a fight, unless it has actually abandoned me. If my faith is not genuine, there is no need to wrestle with the sovereignty (control) of God, since I have chosen to live my life any way I desire.

My faith wearies me when it stands up boldly and reminds me that the objective of God is not about me. It's not about my feelings, my opinion, my intellect, my talents, my disposition, or anything else that relates to me. IT'S ALL ABOUT GOD!

Oh, how my faith gets in the way of ME! Sometimes I just want it to be about me. WHAT ABOUT ME? My faith wearies me because it won't let me hide within the confines of my comfort zone. It makes me rise up when I do not feel like being gallant, brave, creative, or persevering.

Yes, my faith does weary me sometimes. However, it is in that state of weariness that I find my joy, my peace, and my assurance that God has not forsaken me in my times of crisis. It is through this weariness that I am constantly made aware of how much I want to please God in my living. It lets me know that I have not grown cold to His touch. I still respond to His voice, and I do not run and hide like Adam did in the Garden of Eden. I realize that I am still active in wrestling against the flesh that makes me want to trust me more than God, but this weariness produces a peaceful resolve within me that God is working within the circumstances that I find myself and intensifies in me a need for me to remove myself so God can work it out. This spiritual fatigue cues me to the reality that I am working too hard to refurbish something only God can repair.

Many times we see our faith as a *"get out of trouble free card."* We believe that faith is designed to keep the troubles of life away from us. This is not the case. Instead, it is to prevent us from giving up when the desire to do so is so great. For it is only by the grace of God that more tragedy has not occurred in our lives. Our faith in God won't allow us to turn to a source other than God for the things that only God can do. It simply won't allow us to have more trust in someone or something else.

My faith wearies me sometimes because it is stronger than my feelings, stronger than my anger, stronger than my fears, and stronger than my theology. As with all of us, it often overwhelms me when I want control of my situations. It is not something to be afraid of, but rather something to embrace because it lets you know that you are still in touch with God in an intimate way. My faith really helped me to understand that on an everyday basis it will get in the way of my method of operations and cause me to go back to the drawing board of thought to see if I am in line with God's Word. My faith won't allow me to get away with treating God any type of way. My faith makes me stop and ponder the goodness of God and how much I owe Him for his love and favor towards me.

I am glad that my faith shakes me in ways that ultimately make me tired of repeatedly making the same mistakes. My faith does not weary me because it is not authentic, but rather, because it's active and alive. For that, I am truly glad that my faith wearies me.

When My Faith
Makes Me Weary

My faith makes me weary
Only because
I wrestle with logic
Teamed with my flaws

They gnaw at my patience
When God makes me wait
Yet His humbling brilliance
Reminds me how great

He is, that I serve
Who lingers so close
Hears in an instant
And grants me repose

He reminds me my faith
Must often be tested
He frequently states
How much He invested

In my soul's salvation
His blood dropped on the cross
Like divine perspiration
He died for the lost

So I live now by faith
Though my path may get dreary
My time's never wasted
When my faith makes me weary

It's just keeping me rooted
In God's Holy purpose
His love's never muted
It comes to the surface

So to God be the glory
In all that I do
When my faith
makes me weary
Oh God, I seek you.

By Jake Gaines Jr.

Chapter 8

My Faith Will Take Me Where My Ability Can't

Faith is taking the first step even when you can't see the whole staircase…Martin Luther King

We offer God our abilities as if they are separate from his love and grace. We act as though we are responsible for our own abilities and can, therefore, dole them out to God as we so choose. Don't you think it's time for us to recognize that our abilities are simply the results of God pouring from His storehouse into us so that we can offer His gift back to Him? We are enabled because He is able.

I find myself in awe of the abilities that various people in the kingdom of God possess. I have met people from all occupations, who have tremendous drive and fortitude to accomplish marvelous feats. Some people have overcome tremendous odds to achieve very lofty goals. I have been in the presence of some of the most intelligent, charismatic, beautiful, witty, and extremely creative individuals. Yet, for many these are not the only common traits they may share with each other. It appears, when it comes to sharing these abilities in the kingdom of God, they often want the authority to do as they please, when they please, if one wishes to garner their gifts. It is as if God's purpose and objective ceases to be the priority of their journey. *They erroneously believe that ability is the same as authority.*

It often irritates me to see how so many people believe that their ability to accomplish can take them further than their faith in God, especially in the kingdom of God. I'm into my 24th year as a Pastor, and it is mind boggling to me how people proportion the quality of their individual talents and abilities with the authority to use them as they please. This may work in the secular environment, looking out for yourself, but it simply causes a ball of confusion in the kingdom of God. The kingdom of God is not a competition but a family. We do not compete nor compare. We are servants who come to offer ourselves and our resources to God. If God has blessed us with physical and/or cognitive abilities, He should be the first one to be offered them. The problem is that we don't just freely offer God our abilities. Rather, we have the unmitigated gall to barter with God using the very gifts and abilities He has given us as bartering chips. I know. I was once the best at this foolish art, as if I had so much to offer God that He had no alternative.

We literally attempt to use these gifts to our personal advantage to get what we want. We don't mind giving God what we have to offer as long as He rewards us with the proper recognition or position that feeds our insatiable egos. We will literally use God's gift of ability to mask an ulterior motive to promote ourselves. We hone our skills and abilities, but it is not usually for God's glory, but for ours. I wonder how many people sit in our congregations with various types of abilities that could promote the Kingdom of God, but will not offer them until the right opportunity presents itself, the opportune time that promotes their personal agenda.

I believe that God provides, within a specific congregation over a certain period of time, all of the necessary resources He needs for His kingdom to progress.

He simply wants people to humble themselves and offer up their gifts and their resources.

I am often astonished at how much energy we give to our employers while we simultaneously offer God the crumbs of our life after everything else has been taken care of. What makes us think that God is pleased with that? The hours we spend in preparation to get to our jobs, and then in performing them with excellence, far exceeds any time that we offer to God. Think about how much time you invest in just trying to survive on your job, just attempting to make things better for you and your family. Of course these numbers will vary depending on your particular situation, but you will get the idea. Look at how much of our time the job requires of us.

1. 6-8 hours of sleep
2. 1-2 hours of travel time (to & from)
3. 8 hours of actual work

Fifteen to eighteen hours of your life are dedicated to the work place daily. This is not a criticism, simply an observation. We have to work to maintain our lives and support our families. We all understand that. The problem, however, is the free time that we do have, which I know is limited, is sadly and infrequently focused on God. How are your prayer sessions and Bible studies?

There always seems to be problems and higher priorities that need to be dealt with that hinder us from communing with God or attending church and being a consistent participant for God. Have you ever pondered the idea of focusing more on God and letting God deal with the issues of your life? The Bible gives us considerable insight into this problem.

Haggai 1:2-7 (NIV)

2 This is what the LORD Almighty says: "These people say, 'The time has not yet come for the LORD's house to be built.'"

3 Then the word of the LORD came through the prophet Haggai: 4 "Is it a time for you yourselves to be living in your paneled houses, while this house remains a ruin?"

5 Now this is what the LORD Almighty says: "Give careful thought to your ways. 6 You have planted much, but have harvested little. You eat, but never have enough. You drink, but never have your fill. You put on clothes, but are not warm. You earn wages, only to put them in a purse with holes in it."

7 This is what the LORD Almighty says: "Give careful thought to your ways. 8 Go up into the mountains and bring down timber and build the house, so that I may take pleasure in it and be honored," says the LORD. 9 "You expected much, but see, it turned out to be little. What you brought home, I blew away. Why?" declares the LORD Almighty. "Because of my house, which remains a ruin, while each of you is busy with his own house. 10 Therefore, because of you the heavens have withheld their dew and the earth its crops. 11 I called for a drought on the fields and the mountains, on the grain, the new wine, the oil and whatever the ground produces, on men and cattle, and on the labor of your hands."

There is no question that our individual abilities play a major part in the quality of our lives. It is God's design that you use your abilities. However, it is not in lieu of your responsibilities to Him, but in tandem. These elements of your life should work in concert with one another, regardless of how smart you are or how much money you make. Your ability will never take you as far as your faith in God can.

Aren't you tired of wondering how you are going to make it? Doesn't it just weary you to work so diligently for so little return for your effort? It's just one bad report after another as it relates to the economy of this day, Wow! When will it end? It won't, until we get back to walking by faith and not by sight. The wealthy worry about their wealth as much as poor people worry about their poverty. What I see is discouraging, but what I know about God… is a joy to my heart.

Psalms 30:5 says

"For his anger lasts only a moment,
but his favor lasts a lifetime;
weeping may remain for a night,
but rejoicing comes in the morning."

I know that this is true; however, sometimes one wonders. How long is the night?

It's time to take our future back by putting it in the hands of the one who controls it, God. Our government is doing the best it knows how. We have capable people everywhere. We have the smartest of the smart, the brightest of the bright, the most loyal of the loyal, and yet we are steeped in frustration and dead ends.

I am *"soooooo"* happy that my faith in God is genuine, though, unfortunately not perfect. Faith will take me where my ability can not. Ability is always looking around for a new idea, a new approach, and innovation because knowledge is power. However, the weakness in man's ability is constantly being exposed. When many people have to suffer for a few to prosper, it is not by God's design. Think of how many people, educated through our best universities, well trained, highly experienced, or all of the above who cannot find work because of this depressed economy.

In spite of the ability of man, he finds himself being pummeled with the problems of life, without a solution in sight. God has a unique way of showing us that we are helpless without His guidance. When will we finally see that trusting God is our only viable solution? How much do we have to endure before the reality sets in?

This must begin with us as individuals, and then we must teach our family. This way of life will become a part of our communities and will grow from there as God honors our trust.

Faith does not have to look around and peruse the circumstances that surround it because it is not fueled by sight. Faith merely moves forward with its blinders on, with God as the focal point. Faith is neither governed by what it sees nor hindered by the obstacles that stand in its way. Faith just plows through knowing that nothing can hinder its progress because it is Christ-centered. The individual abilities of one person can be offset by the superior abilities of another. Faith can be utilized no matter what arena of life you've found or individual abilities you may possess.

Abilities are limited to the expertise that accompanies them, but faith is undaunted in its quest because it solely depends on the power of God. *That which* rises above our heads still falls below the feet of Jesus. Most of our frustration is the fallout from us living independently from God. When I think about the major problems in my life, they always seem to be the result of me doing my own thing without consulting God in my endeavors. It's those dangerous times in my life when I feel that my ability will take me further than my faith.

It is my faith in God that gives me the authority to go beyond my capabilities. It is my faith in God that gives the authority to tear down the barriers that prohibit me from reaching the lofty goals He has for me, that He might get the glory. If I am repeating myself, please forgive me, but *"ability does not give you authority in the kingdom of God."* It is a dangerous thing to go where God has not sent you. It is true arrogance to believe that God owes you victory in whatever you do. God's will, will not send you where God's grace will not sustain you. Just be confident that you are in the will of God.

On the occasions that I am away from my congregation, I leave someone else in charge of worship service or Christian education classes. I always tell my congregation not to leave just because I am not present. Your victory is not in Pastor Gaines but in the word of God. Because I have left Mr. X with the authority to teach the class, then your blessing will come from the Word of God that is in his mouth. Now, you may have more ability than the person who was authorized to teach, but you still don't have the authorization. Therefore, you don't have the power to make a lasting difference. It is my faith in God that gives me authorization to overcome my obstacles, to conquer my enemy, and to be assured of victory in my battles, not my ability.

Pharoah was confident in his ability to bring the Israelites back to Egypt and reestablish their confinement as slaves and free laborers. Pharoah erroneously associated *the ability to do* with *the authority to go*. Certainly he must have thought, if the Israelites can walk across the Red Sea on dry land, so can my army. We will simply do what they did and put one foot in front of the other. We have the same **ability**. This much was true, but what he did not have was the same **authority** from God.

Exodus 14:21-31

> *21 Then Moses stretched out his hand over the sea, and the LORD drove the sea back by a strong east wind all night and made the sea dry land, and the waters were divided. 22 And the people of Israel went into the midst of the sea on dry ground, the waters being a wall to them on their right hand and on their left. 23 The Egyptians pursued and went in after them into the midst of the sea, all Pharaoh's horses, his chariots, and his horsemen. 24 And in the morning watch the LORD in the pillar of fire and of cloud looked down on the Egyptian forces and threw the Egyptian forces into a panic, 25 clogging [2] their chariot wheels so that they drove heavily. And the Egyptians said, "Let us flee from before Israel, for the LORD fights for them against the Egyptians."*
> *26 Then the LORD said to Moses, "Stretch out your hand over the sea, that the water may come back upon the Egyptians, upon their chariots, and upon their horsemen." 27 So Moses stretched out his hand over the sea, and the sea returned to its normal course when the morning appeared. And as the*

> *Egyptians fled into it, the* LORD *threw [3] the Egyptians into the midst of the sea.* 28 *The waters returned and covered the chariots and the horsemen; of all the host of Pharaoh that had followed them into the sea, not one of them remained.* 29 *But the people of Israel walked on dry ground through the sea, the waters being a wall to them on their right hand and on their left.*
>
> 30 *Thus the* LORD *saved Israel that day from the hand of the Egyptians, and Israel saw the Egyptians dead on the seashore.* 31 *Israel saw the great power that the* LORD *used against the Egyptians, so the people feared the* LORD, *and they believed in the* LORD *and in his servant Moses.*

The miraculous highway through the Red Sea for the Israelites, became the coffin for Pharoah's army. They all drowned, never to be seen again. We must be careful not to give *our ability to do,* more authority than it rightfully deserves. Though your abilities are important, a blessing from God, they are only a blessing when you keep them within their proper parameters. Your abilities will never take you where the authorization of your faith can.

Trust God in all your endeavors because He has the power and the authority to assure you of the victory that is in His perfect will. When your abilities get in the way of you hearing the voice of God, take notice. When you rely totally on your ability in lieu of the will of God, take notice. When you feel confident enough to pursue your spiritual endeavors without the need to consult God, take notice. These are warning signs that you have more faith in your ability than you have in God.

People are smarter than they have ever been. They are more creative, more innovative, and more motivated than any other time in history, and yet it appears that they are getting farther away from God than ever before. Man has become addicted to his ability. Everything is about *more,* except our knowledge of God.

I absolutely thank God for the abilities that He has given us. I just wish we were more inclined to reciprocate. We have ridden our abilities off into the plains of oblivion, and we can't seem to find our way back to God. We should feel deeply indebted to God for all that He has done for us. The more knowledgeable we become, the more we are held accountable to God.

Luke:12:47-48

> *47"That servant who knows his master's will and does not get ready or does not do what his master wants will be beaten with many blows. 48But the one who does not know and does things deserving punishment will be beaten with few blows. From everyone who has been given much, much will be demanded; and from the one who has been entrusted with much, much more will be asked.*

I must admit, with much shame, that it took me too long to grasp this truth. Give all that you have to God for His use, and you will want for nothing. You will have wealth (not necessarily money), health, peace and tranquility. God will bless you going out and coming in.

Remember, everything you need cannot be obtained through your abilities or your wealth. Everything you need to make life fulfilling cannot be purchased. Some things are just gifts from God. Trust God, and walk by faith. When your abilities encounter obstacles they can't overcome, your faith will plow right through them.

Faith Can Take Me Anywhere

There are lots of places I may never see
But it does not bring despair
Life has made it clear to me
That faith can take me anywhere

Faith can take me beyond my fears
To heights right next to God
Faith directs me through my tears
His presence I applaud

Faith can take me where friends won't go
For often they are fragile
When circumstances lose their glow
Friendships can unravel

But I stay encouraged through it all
My walk with God in prayer
If I must journey all alone
Then faith can take me anywhere

When there is no courage within me
When by burdens are too hard to bear
When there is no light for me to see
Faith can take me anywhere

So I will never give up my faith
To trust in my ability
I'd rather stand in my Savior's grace
Than to fail in my futility

So stand firmly on your conviction
Don't dare to look elsewhere
It's God voice to which you listen
Because faith can take you anywhere

By Jake Gaines Jr.

■■■

It is my prayer that you have been helped by this book. I hope it will assist you in taking a realistic look at your everyday walk with God. Pray for me as well because each of us needs to scrutinize our faith with complete honesty if we are to progress in our spiritual walk with God. God bless you.

I want to thank everyone who has prayed for me in my endeavors to do God's will. I pray that God will increase your territory and give you the authority to be a blessing to everyone who comes in contact with you. May you be blessed and satisfied in all that you do.

■■■

A Special Thank You

To My Children

    Jaketta (James)
    Jake B. (Marquita)
    Kia

To My Grandchildren

    Jaisen (6yrs)
    Kyla (1 ½ yrs)
    Jaden (10 mths)
    Jaia (2 ½ mths)

To My Sisters
    Audrey and Barbara

To My Stepchildren and Grandchildren

    Leon
        Abrianna (1yr)

    Teneasha
        Destiny (14 yrs)
        Jabari (4 yrs)
        Giovanni (3yrs)

    De Angelo (Erika)

To My Synagogue Church Family

Thank you for allowing me to grow and exercise my gifts. You are such a blessing to me. I pray that God will continue to allow us to grow and magnify His name for many years to come.

In our 24 year relationship, we have shared this walk of faith. There have been so many obstacles to overcome. Through our prayers for one another and our desire to glorify God we have endured.

You have taught me far more than I could have possibly taught you, and for this I am so grateful. I have watched so many grow and unfortunately, I have watched some go, but through it all you have held me up in prayer and supplication. For this reason, and many others, I love you all.

God has a great work for us to do. He has a purpose for us all. Therefore remain steadfast in your walk with God and always remember:

Galatians 6:7-9

"Do not be deceived: God cannot be mocked. A man reaps what he sows. The one who sows to please his sinful nature, from that nature will reap destruction; the one who sows to please the Spirit, from the Spirit will reap eternal life. Let us not become weary in doing good, for at the proper time we will reap a harvest if we do not give up.

LaVergne, TN USA
05 March 2010
175066LV00002B/1/P